DOGS

BEHAVIOR • BREEDS • HEALTH • GROOMING

DOGS

BEHAVIOR • BREEDS • HEALTH • GROOMING

WELDON
OWEN

Published by Weldon Owen Pty Ltd
59–61 Victoria Street, McMahons Point
Sydney, NSW 2060, Australia
Copyright © 2011 Weldon Owen Pty Ltd

Managing Director Kay Scarlett
Publisher Corinne Roberts
Creative Director Sue Burk
Images Manager Trucie Henderson
Senior Vice President, International Sales Stuart Laurence
Sales Manager, North America Ellen Towell
Administration Manager, International Sales Kristine Ravn
Production Director Todd Rechner
Production and Prepress Controller Mike Crowton
Production Controller Lisa Conway
Production Coordinator Nathan Grice

Designer Jacqueline Richards
Editor Kate McAllan
Editorial Assistant Natalie Ryan

ISBN: 978-1-78342-049-0

Printed by 1010 Printing
Manufactured in China

The paper used in the manufacture of this book is sourced
from wood grown in sustainable forests. It complies with the
Environmental Management System Standard ISO 14001:2004

A WELDON OWEN PRODUCTION

CONTENTS

THE DOG IN YOUR LIFE

BECOMING A DOG OWNER

A DOG IS A LOVING, entertaining and loyal companion. Whether he comes with a pedigree or from a pound, he will be a longtime friend. However, he will demand a lot of you because he relies on you for nearly everything—food, water, shelter, exercise, grooming and veterinary care.

The responsibilities of owning a dog are great, but the love and friendship you'll receive are priceless

CHOOSING THE RIGHT DOG

Before becoming a dog owner, make sure that the family is willing to care for your new pet. Feeding, play, exercise, grooming and training are all essential.

It's hard to resist the appeal of a puppy.

Large or small, pedigreed or mixed breed?

Learn as much as you can about different breeds so you can choose wisely. Don't choose an active dog unless you have time and space to give him the exercise he needs. Think about grooming requirements. Long-coated dogs have beautiful thick coats but it takes time and effort to keep them that way. Short-coated dogs need less grooming but tend to shed hair all year round. In general, males have more behavioral problems than females, so families with children may be better with a female as a first-time pet.

A loyal dog is the perfect family companion.

PUPPY OR ADULT?

While puppies are appealing, chewed shoes and housetraining are not for every family. Some people will wisely choose to adopt an older dog.

Don't adopt a dog, whether from a shelter or another family, just because you feel sorry for her. Although many adult dogs make wonderful pets, some have behavioral problems that might not be obvious. But if you choose carefully, an adult dog may be perfect for you.

If you get a puppy, you will have more control over her learning during the first few months of life. If you have children, your puppy will grow up with them, learning to be tolerant and unafraid of children in general.

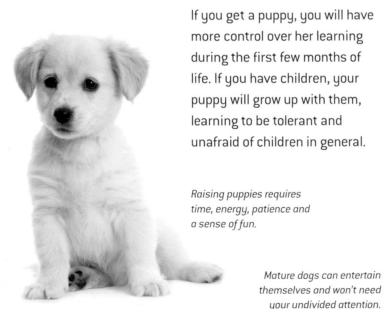

Raising puppies requires time, energy, patience and a sense of fun.

Mature dogs can entertain themselves and won't need your undivided attention.

14

PUREBRED OR MIXED BREED?

Although all dogs vary, purebreds tend to have distinct appearances and are genetically predisposed to behave in certain, predictable ways.

Whether purebred or mixed breed, a dog will be a friend for life if well cared for.

Their breeding has been monitored for centuries, and their ancestry has been studied. All that history means that when you decide on a purebred, you'll have a good idea of the looks, character, size and behavior of the dog you are getting.

The mutt is a lovable hybrid. Because mixed-breed puppies are usually unplanned, a disproportionate number of them wind up in shelters or for sale at low cost—or none at all. But you're not sacrificing quality. Your mixed-breed dog will make a devoted companion, and he can be trained to behave as well as any purebred.

A purebred Border Collie is smart, eager to please and is good with children.

WHERE TO GET A DOG

There are many ways to acquire a dog. Whether it's a purebred or a mixed breed, you want to maximize the chances of her being a perfect match for both of you.

If you're looking for a purebred, it's wise to visit several breeders before making your choice. But an animal shelter is often the first choice for would-be dog owners. This way you can give an unwanted dog a good home.

Shelters are not the exclusive domain of mixed-breed dogs; purebreds show up as well. To give them a second chance, breed rescue clubs provide foster homes to purebreds that have been surrendered to a shelter or abandoned.

A purebred dog can be expensive. Choose a reputable breeder to get your money's worth.

The best place to find a mixed-breed dog is your local animal shelter or pound.

A HEALTHY PUPPY

If you have decided that you have the time and patience for a puppy, you want to make sure you choose a pup that's going to be fit and healthy.

While there's no way to guarantee that your new puppy will never fall ill, you can reduce the chances by checking for certain signs before you make your choice.

Skin
Pull apart his hair to check that his skin is smooth and free of parasites. Its color will range from pink to black to spotted, depending on what type of dog he is. Check that there are no scabs, lumps or pimples.

Anus
Make sure his anus is clean and dry, not red or irritated.

Legs
Check that he moves freely when he walks and runs. He should put even weight on all four legs.

Ears
His ears should be free of discharge, excessive wax and odor.

Eyes
His eyes should be bright, shiny and expressive, with little or no discharge, watering or redness. The eyelashes should not touch the eyeball.

Coat
His coat should be glossy and clean, without excessive oil or dandruff. It will feel shorter and thinner than the coat of an adult dog. There should be little or no shedding when stroked. His belly will usually be hairless.

Nose
His nose will be moist and cool. It should not be running.

Mouth
Pull back his lips to see that his gums are either pink or pigmented, with around 23 white teeth (depending on his age).

PREPARING FOR A NEW DOG

To a dog, a house and yard are full of attractions, and they can easily get themselves into trouble. Before your dog moves in, make sure your home is safe for her.

Dog-proofing is a lot like child-proofing—it means removing anything that may be a danger to your pet, or at risk of being broken. If you have a yard, check that the fencing is secure enough to keep your dog inside. For a small dog, a fence that is 4 feet (1.2 m) high should be adequate, while a 6-foot (1.8 m) fence will hold most large dogs. Remember that dogs such as terriers can dig under a fence, so make sure it is secured.

Keep your dog safe inside a securely fastened fence.

Your new dog will need a bed of her own so that she feels secure.

SETTLING IN

The early days may require some patience. But once your dog has settled in, you'll wonder how you ever got on without him.

When you bring your new dog home, he will probably be confused and apprehensive. It can take a shelter dog a few weeks to adjust and feel secure enough to relax. Give your dog time and a gentle, reassuring approach. Resist the temptation to show off your new dog to visitors until he has settled in. Get him used to you and your family first, before letting him meet strangers. Teach your children to be gentle and quiet around him, especially if he's a puppy. Always supervise them when they are playing together.

With care and love, your new dog will soon feel at home.

Puppies thrive on lots of attention from their new family.

A traveling pen or crate is a good investment. Buy one large enough to fit your puppy when he becomes a fully grown dog.

This puppy enjoys a bath—it's fun and part of her grooming routine.

RAISING A PUPPY

Pups learn by repetition and consistency, so establish a routine that will help your puppy to make sense of her home and what you want from her.

The things your puppy learns between seven and 14 weeks of age will determine her personality. Growing puppies have greater nutritional needs than older dogs and must be fed more often. Until your puppy is about four or five months old, feed her three times a day with a reputable brand of dog food.

Your puppy needs to get used to people, places and things so she can learn how to live happily with all that goes on around her. Take her out and introduce her to new situations and experiences. Make everything you do a positive learning experience.

Puppies and children are a natural fit, but both need to learn the boundaries.

Ensure your puppy has a comfortable collar before starting leash training.

THE RESPONSIBLE OWNER

A dog's love is a privilege, and with it comes genuine responsibility. Your dog depends on you and deserves the best care and guidance you can provide.

It is your responsibility to feed your dog a balanced diet and to provide water at all times. Daily exercise or play will keep him fit and stop him from getting lonely, anxious or bored and developing behavioral problems. You must also provide regular medical care and vaccinations to prevent the transmission of diseases to people and other dogs. Washing and grooming your dog will keep him looking good and control skin parasites, which can lead to health problems that can be passed on to people. You must also collect his droppings from all public places and dispose of them in an appropriate way.

Well-trained dogs make the best pets, so take them to obedience school from an early age.

Be a responsible owner—always clean up after your dog.

UNDERSTANDING YOUR DOG

NO MATTER HOW INTELLIGENT and alert your dog may be, she has ways of seeing, hearing and thinking about the world that are totally different from yours. The key to a happy life together is to learn to read your dog's behavior and to become aware of how she interprets yours.

With understanding and good training, the bond between humans and dogs can be rewarding for both.

LEADERS AND FOLLOWERS

In the dog world, you are either a leader or a follower. This pack mentality comes from the wolves that are the ancestors of today's dogs.

Wolves rely on their leader for their survival. Even if a wolf is not top dog, he is a link in the chain of command. It's the same with a dog. His instinct is to find out where he stands.

Like their wolf ancestors, today's domestic dogs are pack animals.

The dog family includes the endangered African hunting dog.

Most dogs are followers. They want to please their human pack so they can get plenty of positive attention. But dogs need a social structure with a leader and clear hierarchy. If no one takes the role of leader, your dog will fill the gap. He may display dominant behavior such as ignoring your commands or even threatening you.

Dogs look to their leader for guidance and reassurance. They expect you to be "top dog."

HOW DOGS COMMUNICATE

Dogs are expert communicators who use an elaborate repertoire of body postures, sounds and scent to get their message across to other dogs.

Unlike humans, dogs do not camouflage their emotions, so watching them act and react together will give you a good idea of what they are saying. When dogs meet, the first thing they do is establish rank. The anal sacs underneath dogs' tails contain glandular secretions that vary in composition from dog to dog, so the nose-to-rear-end method of greeting works well for them. With one sniff a dog can learn the gender, age, sexual status, attitude and authority of another. He'll know whether they've met before, and what their relationship is likely to be.

Rolling over is a sign of submission that is learned in puppyhood.

Barks, whines, howls and growls all have a place in canine language.

Sniffing is an important way for dogs to establish rank and status.

BODY LANGUAGE

Dogs are tactile animals who use their bodies to express affection, possession, fear or rank. As a general rule, submissive dogs usually contract while dominant dogs expand.

On guard duty *This Border Collie's full attention is on something out of the ordinary. It's her job to alert her owner, so her stance is confident, her eyes focused. She'll continue to bark until her owner assures her that everything is now okay.*

Yawning People usually yawn when they are tired or bored, but among dogs, yawning is often a signal that they're feeling stressed. A good yawn briefly lowers their blood pressure and helps them to stay calm.

The play-bow This is the way your dog invites either you or another dog to join in a game. When a dog wants to play, she will lower the front half of her body to the ground. The rear end will be left pointing in the air in what looks like a bow, and the tail will be waving madly in anticipation. The head may be lowered, with the mouth and lips relaxed, and the dog may pant. Sometimes she will give a high-pitched bark and prick her ears up alertly.

37

BODY LANGUAGE

Sideways look *A stare isn't always a sign of aggression. Dogs look out of the corners of their eyes when they're being coy or asking to play. It's a polite way of expressing interest without being pushy.*

Fear of thunderstorms *Dogs' senses are much sharper than ours. Because they hear higher and lower frequencies than we do, the sound of thunder is more intense and scary. When thunderstorms are raging, this Australian Shepherd follows his natural instinct and looks for shelter in an enclosed place, such as under the bed, where he will feel safer.*

Tucked tail Submissive, anxious or frightened dogs tuck their tails between their legs. The farther the tail is tucked, the stronger the feelings. A very frightened dog will tuck his tail right under his stomach. But even when the tail is tucked, the tip will wag a bit, which displays his stress.

Tail wagging Although a wagging tail usually indicates a friendly dog, that's not always the case. Dogs also wag their tails when they are scared, agitated or unsure. A frightened dog may wag his tail low and between his legs as he decides whether to fight, flee or go belly up. An aggressive, angry dog may wag his tail high while he chases or even attacks.

COMMUNICATING WITH YOUR DOG

Just as your dog's body language indicates her moods and reactions, your body, face, voice and actions are sending signals to your dog.

A well-trained dog will love, obey and enjoy the company of a child.

Dogs' senses are incredibly sharp but their interpretations of human movements and facial expressions are limited. No matter how attentive dogs are, it's impossible for them to think like a person. Except for a few vocal commands, dogs mainly respond to intonations and body language. Base your commands on her language, and consider how she interprets your own behavior.

Dogs respect those who are self-assured and confident. If you adopt a confident posture and an enthusiastic attitude your dog will know that your commands are right for her—and she'll obey them.

Good communication will have long-term benefits for both dog and owner.

TRAINING YOUR DOG

EVERY DOG NEEDS to be taught basic good manners. Not only does it ensure his safety, but it will also give you peace of mind. Remember that a dog is a pack animal and he will expect to follow rules and obey a leader. It is vital that your dog recognizes you as his leader.

Is chewing acceptable? If you set the boundaries, both you and your dog will be happier.

HOUSETRAINING A PUPPY

Stay calm! Your puppy is an intelligent animal who will soon learn where—and where not—to go.

When a puppy enters your life, housetraining becomes a priority. Like their ancestors, the wolves, dogs will not dirty their eating and sleeping areas.

If you follow this instinct for cleanliness, your puppy can be housetrained with a minimum of mopping up. Assign your puppy an area for her toilet spot. In most cases, this will be a place in your yard. Once she's at her spot, allow her some time to explore. Then use a key phrase to encourage her. When she is successful, praise her, using your key phrase so that she will begin to associate it with elimination.

A crate can be your puppy's own cozy place. She won't soil where she sleeps.

House-training won't take place overnight and a few mishaps are to be expected at first.

Your puppy will need to go 10—20 minutes after eating, and straight after walking, exercising or drinking.

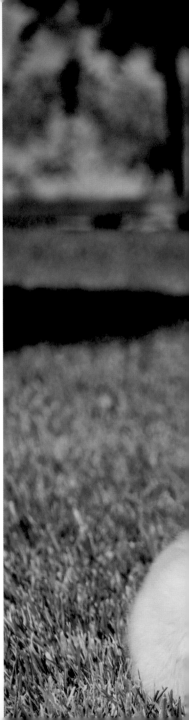

COLLAR AND LEASH

When you put a collar on your puppy for the first time, he will scratch, yelp and roll on the ground to try and take it off. But you do need to persist.

Before leash training your dog, ensure he has a comfortable collar. The right collar will not hurt him—it's just a strange, new sensation. He will soon be used to it and ready to begin his lessons. The collar should fit snugly. Don't buy a collar that is too big, thinking that he will grow into it—a collar that is too loose will slip off easily and be useless.

It's standard practice to stand to your dog's right while he is on a leash. Hold the leash in your right hand and use the left hand to reach down to him.

A well-trained dog will associate his leash with a walk and fun in the park.

Make sure you buy a well-fitting collar. Large dogs will outgrow several.

TEACHING "SIT"

Most dogs learn to sit very easily, but you have to keep them practicing until they can consistently associate the command with the action.

By using a food treat, you can easily get your dog to sit. Repeat the process below six to eight times, praising him every time he performs the task.

While training takes time and effort, a well-trained dog will be a lifelong companion.

1 *With your dog facing you, hold a food reward between your fingers and thumb with your palm facing up, in front of his nose.*

2 *Then raise your hand up and slightly back over his head. Say "Sit" once as you do this. As your dog follows the treat with his eyes and head, he will sit down.*

3 *Once he does this, praise your dog, saying "Good sit," and give him the food reward.*

TEACHING "COME"

A dog that will reliably respond to a call to "Come" will always be safe. This task may be difficult to teach, but a couple of tips will make the command easier to instill.

Never call your dog and then punish her. Also, take care not to call her away from something fun, like chewing a toy.

1 Stand close to your dog with a food reward in your hand.

2 Back up a short distance, wiggle the treat and say "Come."

Teaching your dog to come when called will keep her safe when danger looms.

3 As your dog approaches, say "Good come" and give her a treat when she gets to you.

TEACHING "STAY"

Teaching your dog to stay on command may avoid a disaster, especially if you live in a busy urban area where a passing car can so easily hit a moving dog.

However, getting your dog to stay can be a difficult task, so it will be a lot easier if you aim for small successes, rather than long stays. Initially, reward your puppy with food and praise if she does not move for five seconds. Then gradually increase the duration of the stay.

1 With your puppy in a sit, place your hand, palm open, in front of her face.

Teaching your dog to stay on command could save her life.

2 Say "Stay" in a firm voice as you back away a few paces.

3 If your puppy does not move for five seconds, reward her with food and praise.

TEACHING "HEEL"

"Heel" means "stay by my side when we go walking." Some dogs are natural heelers, while others require a lot of training to obey this important command.

"Watch Me"
With your dog facing you, point to your eyes (holding a treat to get his attention if need be) and say "Watch me." Try to maintain eye contact for about 10 seconds. Release and reward him. Repeat frequently at various locations and around different distractions.

"Heel," or the follow command, is an extension of the "Watch me" command. Repeat this command several times and add the command "Heel." At first, move only short distances, but gradually move farther and for longer periods as the dog learns to stay with you.

A well-trained dog will stay by your side on a walk or a run.

1 With your dog in a sit by your side, say "Watch me" and make eye contact.

2 Take a couple of steps forward and say "Heel." If your dog is really watching and tries to maintain eye contact, he will move with you.

3 Stop, and when your dog also stops say "Good heel."

TEACHING "FETCH"

1 Toss a toy or ball a short distance. When the puppy looks to the toy, say "Fetch."

Fetch is a fun game for both you and your puppy, and will provide your pet with much of the exercise he requires. A little patience is needed to get the message across.

Some dogs will fetch more eagerly than others as certain breeds, such as retrievers, naturally pick things up and carry them around. The hard part is getting them to give them back.

Most dogs enjoy a lively game of fetch with their owner.

2 A the puppy picks it up, say "Good dog" and "Come."

3 To get your puppy to drop the toy on command, hold up another toy and say "Drop it."

4 When your puppy drops the toy, praise him and quickly throw the new toy. His main reward in this game is that the game continues.

EXERCISE

Providing your dog with a daily workout is a key responsibility. It could be a long jog, a steady walk, or simply playing chase and fetch around the apartment.

Regular exercise is essential for your dog's physical wellbeing. It will prevent him from becoming overweight and will also provide a lot of fun.

Exercise is also essential for your dog's emotional health. The well-exercised dog is less likely to get bored and develop troublesome traits, such as persistent barking, chewing and destructive digging. Exercise also causes the release of endorphins in the brain. These chemicals give your dog a great feeling of wellbeing—a natural "high."

If you are unable to exercise your dog daily yourself, employ the services of a dog walker.

A game of catch is great exercise for an active dog— and for his owner as well.

DEALING WITH AGGRESSION

For dogs, aggression is just another form of communication. Similar to human insecurity and anger, aggression is a dog's way of setting boundaries.

Territorial dogs must be handled carefully and given firm, but not harsh, training.

In the wild, dogs depended on aggression to protect their resources—such as food—from other dogs, and also to protect the pack from intruders and themselves from bodily harm. What's acceptable in the wild, however, is not acceptable in your home.

The best way to deal with aggressive behavior is to prevent it in the first place. Establish yourself as leader from the outset. You can do this by setting rules that are humanely but consistently enforced. If you must reprimand your dog, a firm, verbal rebuke is enough.

Dousing fighting dogs with a jet of water will startle them and make them break up long enough for you to separate them.

DEALING WITH BARKING

If it's a dog, it barks—to communicate, to indicate excitement or fear, or to warn of intruders. But barking can be annoying for owners and neighbors alike.

Dogs may bark because they are lonely or bored—company and exercise are vital.

While you will never stop your dog from barking altogether, you can at least get the behavior under control by using methods such as the "Quiet" command. But first you must determine why your dog is barking so much.

1 To train your dog to stop barking, you must first get him to start. Speak in an excited tone, or ring the doorbell. When he barks, tell him "Good bark" and give him a treat. Keep doing this until the command alone sets him off. It's now time to teach him to stop barking on command.

2 Give the command to get him barking. As he pauses between barks, hold a treat over his nose and say, "Quiet."

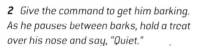

3 He can't bark and chew at the same time, so he'll swap one activity for the other. Keep practicing until he stops barking when you tell him "Quiet."

CHEWING AND DIGGING

Dogs get a lot of fun and satisfaction from chewing. It is a natural activity and helps exercise their jaws and clean their teeth. Puppies chew as a way to explore their world.

A few rubber chew toys will keep most dogs happy.

Chewing is normal behavior for dogs. The trick is to ensure your dog chews only the right things.

However, dogs who spend a lot of time alone will sometimes chew as a way of dispelling loneliness, anxiety or boredom. Don't try to stop the activity—just direct the behavior to more appropriate objects, such as ropes, balls and chew toys, and find ways to relieve your dog's tension.

Dogs also love to dig. Some breeds, such as terriers, are genetically programmed to dig. If you catch your dog digging where he shouldn't, tell him "No!" and distract him with a toy. You can also deter him by placing heavy bricks over that area. Wrap wire mesh securely around plants you want to protect.

Your dog may be digging to expend energy, so take her for a lively daily walk.

FEEDING AND HEALTH CARE

FEEDING YOUR DOG a nutritious and balanced diet is one of the most important things you can do to keep her healthy and happy. Good preventative health care should begin in puppyhood. Knowing basic first aid treatments in an emergency could save your dog's life.

If your dog does get hurt, she will appreciate your care and attention—and professional treatment when needed.

THE HEALTHY DOG

Check over your dog on a regular basis. Start by looking at his ears, then move on to his eyes, nose, mouth, body, legs, tail and paws.

Anus
Clean, dry and lump-free; no irritation; anal sacs unswollen; fur unmatted; parasite-free

Skin
Smooth, clean, dry, pliable, odorless; parasite-free. Colored black, brown, pink or spotted, depending on breed

Ears
Pink, smooth, glossy, odorless; slightly oily

Nose
Cool and moist; free of discharge; not crusty or cracked; no loss of pigmentation

Teeth
White; no buildup of tartar; no broken or missing teeth

Gums and tongue
Bright pink (or tinged with black, depending on breed); moist; never bleeding; no lumps

Eyes
Clear and bright; the pupils equal size; membranes a healthy pink

Breath
Inoffensive

Breathing
Quiet, regular and comfortable. Should pant only when hot, excited or stressed

Feet
No mats or debris between toes

Pads
No cuts or blisters

Nails
Trimmed; just touching the ground

Ribs
Not too prominent; nor covered with thick padding of fat

Coat
Clean, shiny, unmatted; no excessive shedding; no bald spots

NUTRITIONAL NEEDS

The six basic nutrients required by all living things are proteins, carbohydrates, minerals, vitamins, fats and plenty of fresh, clean water.

A dog's individual requirements will determine how much of these nutrients she should have, depending on her age, state of health and lifestyle. Whether you feed your dog at regular times or make food available throughout the day depends on the type of food you feed, your dog's tendency to overeat, her age and health. Most adult dogs can sustain their nutrient levels on one meal a day.

A dog will experience her greatest growth in her first year, so she'll need more high-quality animal-derived protein and a specially formulated puppy food.

Keep your dog fit by not overfeeding her.

It's best to feed dogs from individual bowls according to each one's size and needs.

KINDS OF DOG FOOD

Commercial dog foods come in three basic types: dry, semi-moist and moist canned. There are also three quality levels: generic, popular name-brand and premium.

Specially formulated dog treats provide good nutrients but should be given sparingly.

What you choose to feed your dog is up to you. The difference is in the ingredients, palatability, cost and convenience. To get the balance of nutrients right for your dog—taking into account his breed, age, size and levels of activity—you may need to feed him a mixture of types.

Biscuits are a tasty treat for an obedient dog, but don't give them out too often.

Treats are a great way to reward your dog for learning tricks and commands. But many snacks and treats are high in calories and not nutritionally balanced. Like all good things, they should be given in moderation, especially if your dog is overweight.

Whatever you feed your dog, make sure it contains high-quality ingredients such as animal protein.

HEALTH CARE BASICS

The best way to keep your dog healthy is to notice the first signs of a possible problem before it becomes serious and deal with it quickly.

Trimming your dog's nails will make it easier for her to walk in comfort. Your vet can do this regularly.

In order to do this, give her a complete once-over every week. Once you know what to look for, you'll know right away whether you need to be concerned. Never be afraid to seek your vet's help if you need it.

Poor dental hygiene can lead to mouth infections and gum diseases.

There are some common diseases to which all dogs are susceptible. But vaccines will prevent your dog from contracting many of these illnesses—including rabies, parvovirus, distemper and Lyme disease. Combined with a monthly oral medication to prevent heartworm, these annual vaccinations are a vital investment in your dog's good health.

No one knows your dog better than you, and a ten-minute checkup every week will help keep her healthy.

HOME CARE

For minor injuries and ailments, treating your dog at home is not only less expensive and more convenient—he'll be a lot less stressed if he is in his own home.

Your dog needs professional attention after an injury.

Giving a liquid medicine Use a dropper or syringe to draw up the correct dose of medicine. Insert the end of the dropper or syringe in the side of your dog's mouth and gently squeeze in the liquid. Work slowly, giving him plenty of time to swallow.

An Elizabethan collar will prevent your dog from licking or scratching infected skin.

Giving pills Put the pill between your forefinger and thumb and use your other fingers to push down the lower jaw. Place it in the center of the tongue, as far back as you can. Hold your dog's mouth shut until he licks his nose—this indicates that he has swallowed. If he's reluctant to swallow, massage his throat to encourage him.

Many health problems respond well to medication. It's important to give the prescribed dose.

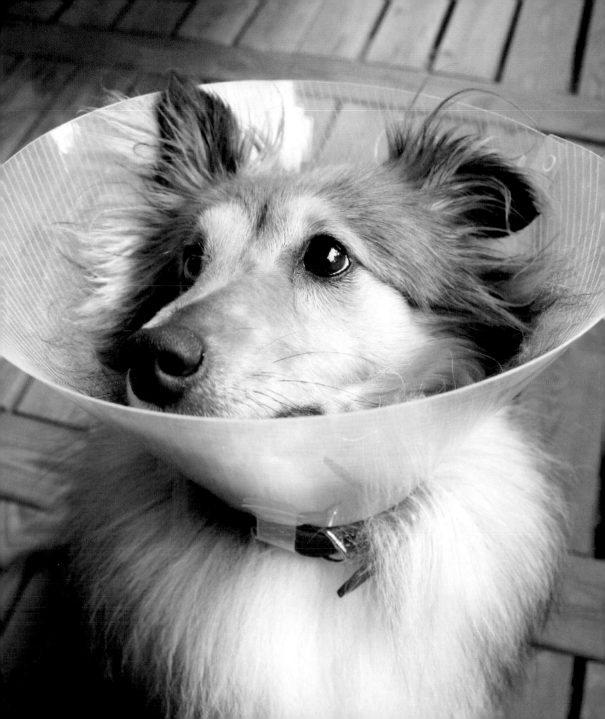

SKIN CARE

Skin conditions are probably the most common canine medical problems that vets treat. The problem can be as mild as dry skin or as serious as a severe infection.

Signs of skin disease include itchiness, dandruff, hair loss, crusting, redness or lumps. Severe itching, scratching, rubbing and licking can lead to skin infections. If your dog is scratching, suspect fleas or lice—but if there's no sign of parasites, consult your vet. Some dogs scratch because they are allergic to things they have touched, eaten or inhaled.

If licking is confined to one area, a "hot spot" can develop. Bacteria spread rapidly among the hair follicles in the irritated area, causing bald patches of inflamed skin. These will heal on their own if they are kept clean.

This hairless Chinese Crested has special needs, but all dogs benefit from attention to their skin.

Be aware of excessive scratching, which may signal a skin problem.

A healthy coat can withstand mud, dirt and extremes of temperature— but a bath will prevent irritation.

WEIGHT PROBLEMS

Obesity is the number-one nutrition-related disease in dogs. Some breeds put on weight easily and require special attention to their feeding needs.

The Bulldog is a naturally large breed but, as with all dogs, care is needed not to overfeed them.

Sometimes a metabolic disease, such as hypothyroidism, triggers obesity. However, most overweight dogs simply eat too much and exercise too little. If your dog has a weight problem, your vet can design a weight-reduction program. It may simply be a question of changing her food to meet a lower calorific target. Try dividing your dog's daily ration into two or three portions. More frequent feedings will keep hunger pangs at bay.

Overweight dogs have a lower quality of life, and a shorter lifespan, than those of normal weight.

Regular exercise is a vital part of any weight-loss program. Starting with short sessions of five or ten minutes, try to work up to 30 minutes of active play or brisk walking every day.

AN AGING DOG

A dog that is well cared for can be expected to live for about 12 years. But as dogs age they become more susceptible to a number of health problems.

While some health problems are an inevitable part of aging, others are actually illnesses that can be successfully treated. Contact your vet if you notice a loss of energy or appetite; increased thirst and urination; discharges; sores that won't heal; weight changes; abnormal odors; lumps on the skin; and coughing or sneezing.

Your aging dog may experience problems similar to those caused by senility in people. He may forget his training, or his responses may be slower. New drugs and a retraining program can improve his quality of life.

Older dogs enjoy napping, but regular, gentle exercise helps keep them alert.

Your older dog deserves all your loving care and attention.

EMERGENCY CARE

Knowing how to recognize and react to common emergencies may save your dog's life. But remember, it is vital that you seek immediate veterinary help.

Dogs are curious and adventurous, and can get themselves into all sorts of trouble. Unfortunately, it is common for dogs running free in urban areas to be hit by cars. This traumatic injury can result in lacerations, fractures, shock, bleeding, spinal injuries, internal damage and, sometimes, death.

Carefully lift an injured small dog with both hands and let any fractured limbs dangle freely.

While this situation is best prevented by keeping your dog leashed or confined to a fenced yard, sometimes a dog will escape and be hit despite your best efforts. If your dog is hit by a car, take her to a vet immediately. However, when you move her, do so carefully.

Take your injured dog to the vet as soon as possible to ensure she receives the best professional care.

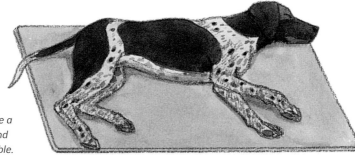

To move a large dog, slide a firm surface under her and move as gently as possible.

WHEN TO VISIT THE VET

You should find a good local vet as soon as you become a dog owner to ensure that your new companion gets the best possible care, in sickness and in health.

Ask your dog-owning friends to recommend a good vet or call your local veterinary association for a referral. At the first visit, your vet will give your puppy a thorough checkup to make sure he is healthy and will set up his regular vaccination schedule.

Puppies are susceptible to life-threatening but easily prevented diseases, such as distemper and parvovirus. Vaccines are given two or three times at three-to-four-week intervals until the puppy is 12 to 14 weeks old. Most vaccines are boosted annually.

Your vet will discuss all the issues you need to understand to care for your dog.

A good vet will provide security for you and your dog.

GROOMING

DOGS KEEP THEMSELVES CLEAN by rubbing and rolling on the ground, and licking and scratching themselves. However, this is often just not enough to meet the human definition of clean. Regular cleaning will keep your dog looking good and make life more pleasant for everyone.

Every dog has different grooming needs, depending on size, shape, hair and coat.

DIFFERENT COATS

To know how best to groom your dog, you need to determine the type of coat he has. All dog coats fit into one of the following categories.

Short double coat
Labradors have this coat, with straight, coarse hair on the outside and a soft, thin coat beneath.

Long coarse coat
The long, human-hairlike quality of this coat makes it one of the more time-consuming coats to groom.

Long silky coat
The coats of breeds such as Yorkshire, Silky and Maltese terriers need to be groomed at least two or three times a week.

Short smooth coat

Pugs, Basenjis and Doberman Pinschers have short, smooth coats. As there is no undercoat, these dogs are probably the easiest to groom.

Short wiry coat

Dogs with short wiry coats have hair that is thick and hard, and somewhat bristly to the touch.

Hairless coat

Since they have little or no hair, dogs such as the Chinese Crested don't require regular brushing. However, they do need frequent baths to keep them clean.

Curly coat

This coat does not shed, so regular brushing and clipping is required to keep the soft curls looking neat.

Long double coat

Samoyeds and Collies have a long, straight and coarse outer coat with a very thick undercoat.

Dog hairbrush

GROOMING YOUR DOG

To keep your dog looking her best, you will need to have the right grooming equipment. There's a wide range of brushes, combs and other grooming tools to choose from.

Start with a gentle massage accompanied with praise. About once a month, do your home health checks. Start grooming from head to toe. Use a flea comb to check for fleas or ticks. Clean any discharge from your dog's eyes with a cotton ball moistened in lukewarm water. If your dog's ears are dirty or there is any sign of discharge, clean the ear flaps and ear openings with a damp cotton ball.

A combined approach—brushing your dog, followed by a thorough combing—will remove huge amounts of excess hair.

A wide-toothed comb will keep your dog's coat silky.

Longhaired dogs, such as this Afghan Hound, require regular grooming to keep them in tip-top shape.

CLIPPING YOUR DOG

Although mastering the art of clipping belongs to the professional groomer, you too can learn to clip your dog and make him look good.

The extent to which you use clippers depends on the type of dog you have, but most dogs benefit from some tidying up. The breed that requires the most clipping is the poodle. Not only is this because of its stylishness, but also because a poodle's coat grows continuously. Show poodles have their hair clipped down to the skin in some places, and fluffed up in others. Unless yours is a show dog, you will be better off keeping your poodle (or any breed that requires clipping) in a simple clip that is easy to maintain.

Pedigreed dogs, especially longhaired breeds, benefit from professional clipping.

Poodles need to be bathed regularly and clipped every six to eight weeks to lighten the weight of their coat.

Clipping a longhaired dog is a professional skill. Show dogs receive special attention to make them look their best.

BATHING YOUR DOG

Most dogs need a bath only once or twice a year. Brushing distributes the natural oils and cleans the coat much better than soap and water.

1 Try to give a bath on a warm day and start early. Thick coats take a long time to dry. First, brush the coat well to get rid of tangles.

2 Use warm water and a shampoo made for dogs or babies. Keep suds and water away from your dog's eyes and ears. It's good to have someone to hold the dog still.

3 Rinse well—don't forget to rinse the feet as soapy residues can make them itch. If possible, use a shower head on a flexible hose. Stand back when your dog shakes herself!

4 Use towels to dry the coat as much as possible. Let your dog run around to warm up. Brush her coat again to dry it quickly.

Washing your dog in an outdoor tub is fun for all.

Dogs will naturally shake themselves dry—but they also enjoy a bit of help.

GUIDE TO BREEDS

HOW TO USE THIS GUIDE

So you want to become the proud owner of a purebred dog? This guide provides details of the most popular breeds to help you decide which dog is best for you.

Temperament
Brief summary of temperament

Grooming
Preferred grooming manner and frequency

Exercise
Type and frequency required

Living conditions
Preferred environment

Watchdog
Brief summary of ability

Size and weight
Average size for males and females. Height is measured from the ground to the shoulder.

♂ = male   ♀ = female

Be aware!
Common health problems that may afflict each breed

Name of breed
As used by the American Kennel Club

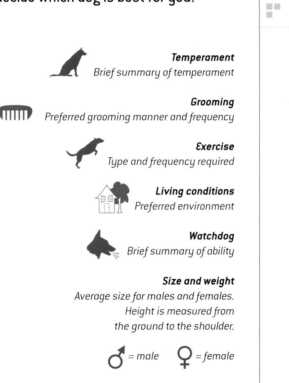

HOUNDS

BASSET HOUND

The mournful face of this gentle, lovable nature. When hunting, it is single-minde a delightful pet in homes where there a

Gentle and loyal	
Weekly brushing, paying attention to ears and feet	
Regular, moderate	
Suited to urban living	
Not a good watchdog	
♂ 12-15 in (30-38 cm) 50-65 lb (23-29 kg)	
♀ 11-14 in (28-36 cm) 45-60 lb (20-27 kg)	

TEMPER

Good-na
Basset
training
an inter
attentic

GROOMI

The sm
and bru
when n
trim toe
regular

★ *These dogs may smell due to skin and ear infections*
★ *Prone to overeating and becoming fat*

288

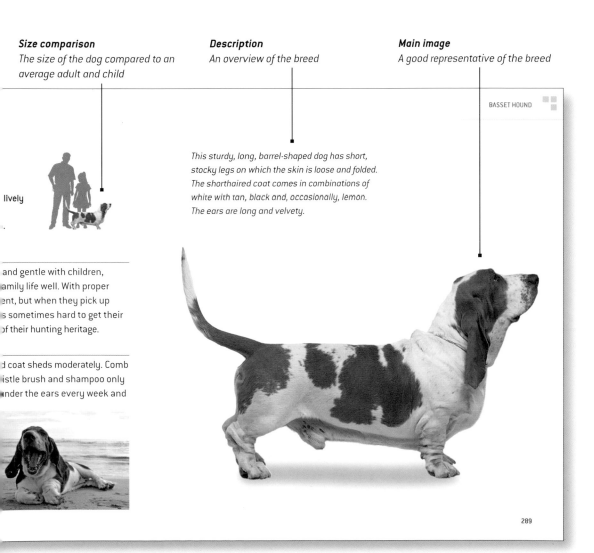

Size comparison
The size of the dog compared to an average adult and child

Description
An overview of the breed

Main image
A good representative of the breed

BASSET HOUND

This sturdy, long, barrel-shaped dog has short, stocky legs on which the skin is loose and folded. The shorthaired coat comes in combinations of white with tan, black and, occasionally, lemon. The ears are long and velvety.

lively

and gentle with children,
amily life well. With proper
ent, but when they pick up
s sometimes hard to get their
of their hunting heritage.

d coat sheds moderately. Comb
istle brush and shampoo only
nder the ears every week and

289

HERDING DOGS

FOR THOUSANDS OF YEARS, herding dogs have been protecting livestock from predators and stopping them straying. They tend to be nimble and intelligent, and have great stamina. Today, many herding dogs are still employed in their traditional roles, while others are kept as pets.

Herding dogs make wonderful pets given sufficient exercise and attention to keep them busy.

SHETLAND SHEEPDOG

The Sheltie is well endowed with both beauty and brains. Intuitive and responsive to its owner's wishes, it makes a charming family pet, becoming deeply attached.

 Obedient, loyal, intelligent

 Regular brushing

 Regular, moderate

 Ideal for apartment living, but needs plenty of exercise

 Good watchdog

 13-15 in (33-38 cm)
14-18 lb (6-8 kg)

12-14 in (30-36 cm)
12-16 lb (5-7 kg)

★ *Excessive barking can be a problem with this breed*

★ *Sensitive to some heartworm preventatives*

TEMPERAMENT

Alert and remarkably intelligent, the sensitive Sheltie likes to feel like part of the family. It is easy to train, but may be shy with strangers.

GROOMING

Shelties are fastidious about cleanliness but are easier to care for than you might expect. Regular brushing is vital. Mist lightly with water then tease out mats, using the comb sparingly. The dense undercoat is shed in spring and fall. The coat readily sheds dirt. Bathe or dry shampoo only when absolutely necessary.

Strong, nimble and lightly built, the Sheltie is fast and jumps well. The most common colors for the long, shaggy coat are sable, blue merle and tricolor. More rarely, it can also come in black with white or tan.

The long, powerful little body is set on short legs. Its coat comes in red, sable, fawn, tan and black, all with or without white. Compared to the Cardigan, the Pembroke's tail is short or is docked very close to the body.

PEMBROKE WELSH CORGI

Long associated with royalty, especially the British monarch, the Pembroke Welsh Corgi is a widely recognized and popular pet. Its neat size and affectionate nature alone recommend it.

 Affectionate, loyal, independent

 Regular brushing

 Regular, gentle

 Ideal for apartment living, but needs plenty of exercise

 Very good watchdog

 ♂ 10-12 in (25-30 cm)
25-30 lb (11-14 kg)

 ♀ 10-12 in (25-30 cm)
24-28 lb (11-13 kg)

★ Heavy shedding twice a year and some year-round shedding

★ Prone to slipped disks as has a long back

TEMPERAMENT

Pembrokes adore children, but because their way of getting sheep or cattle to move is to nip at their heels, they have a tendency to also nip people. This trait should be firmly discouraged from an early age. They are wary of strangers and make very good watchdogs.

GROOMING

The soft, medium-length, water-resistant coat is easy to groom. Comb and brush with a firm bristle brush, and bathe only when necessary. The coat is shed freely twice a year.

CARDIGAN WELSH CORGI

Although it has not attained the widespread popularity of the Pembroke, the Cardigan Welsh Corgi is a great favorite in Wales and in fact predominates in many rural communities.

 Obedient, alert, intelligent

 Regular brushing

 Regular, gentle

 Ideal for apartment living, but needs plenty of exercise

 Very good watchdog

 10-13 in (25-33 cm)
25-30 lb (11-14 kg)

 10-13 in (25-33 cm)
25-30 lb (11-14 kg)

★ These dogs may suffer from spinal problems

★ The breed has some inherited eye disorders

TEMPERAMENT

Intelligent and easy to train, Cardigans make obedient little workers. Like Pembrokes, they should be firmly discouraged from nipping. Because of their tendency to nip, they are not well suited to households with children. Wary of strangers, they make good watchdogs.

GROOMING

The wiry, medium-length, water-resistant coat is easy to groom. Comb and brush with a firm bristle brush, and bathe only when necessary. The coat is shed twice a year.

Tough and fearless, it can run fast on short, well-boned legs. The face is foxlike and the coat comes in any color but pure white. Slightly longer than the Pembroke, the Cardigan has a long, thick tail and larger, more widely spaced ears.

The wiry, medium-sized Puli has a long, dense, water-resistant double coat falling in matted cords, eventually reaching the ground and hiding its legs. The black hair is often reddish or tinged with gray. The tail curls over the back.

PULI

The natural "dreadlocks" worn in such a carefree way by the Puli are an adaptation to protect the animal from extremes of weather. In mature coat, these dogs are an amazing sight.

 Happy, playful, intelligent

 Extensive grooming

 Regular, moderate

 Suited to urban living, but needs plenty of space

 Good watchdog

 16-18 in (41-46 cm)
25-35 lb (11-16 kg)

 14-16 in (36-41cm)
20-30 lb (9-14 kg)

★ *A heavy, waterlogged coat may drag the dog down in water*

★ *Not suited to hot climates*

TEMPERAMENT

Pulis, or more correctly Pulik, are agile, intelligent dogs that respond to training—they are used as police dogs in their native Hungary, where they were originally sheepdogs and guards. They make great companions.

GROOMING

This coat does not shed and is often left in its natural state. Simply separate the strands with your fingers from time to time. The dog can be bathed when necessary, but disturb the cords as little as possible. Clean around the ears and eyes regularly. Some owners prefer to clip their dog and do not allow the coat to cord.

AUSTRALIAN CATTLE DOG

The Australian Cattle Dog, also known as a Heeler, has in its make-up the best characteristics of its several antecedents. If you need a working dog, this is as good as they get.

 Diligent, courageous, loyal

 Minimal

 Regular, vigorous

 Adapts to urban living, but needs plenty of exercise

 Excellent watchdog

 17-20 in (43-51 cm)
32-35 lb (15-16 kg)

 17-19 in (43-48 cm)
30-35 lb (14-16 kg)

TEMPERAMENT

The Australian Cattle Dog is loyal and obedient to its master, but it is something of a one-person dog. Both its guarding and herding instincts are strong and may extend to people and other pets. It may also feel compelled to establish dominance over other dogs.

GROOMING

The coarse, shorthaired, weather-resistant coat needs little care and is easy to groom. Just comb and brush with a firm bristle brush and bathe only when necessary.

★ *Check puppies for any signs of deafness before purchasing*

★ *Needs a lot of exercise or can become bored and destructive*

Not your average pampered pooch, this tough and intelligent, medium-sized dog was bred for hard work. There are two coat colors: speckled blue, with tan or black markings; or speckled red, with dark red markings.

This athletic dog is known for mesmerizing sheep. Its medium-length, double coat mainly comes in black with white. It has feathering on the legs, underbody and tail and a ruff behind the head.

BORDER COLLIE

Ready, willing and able sums up the Border Collie asleep at your feet. You might think you've tired him out, but move a muscle and he'll be instantly alert, ready to learn a new trick.

 Intelligent, cooperative, joyful

 Regular brushing

 Regular, vigorous

 Suits urban living, but needs plenty of space

 Good watchdog

♂ 19-22 in (48-56 cm)
30-45 lb (14-20 kg)

♀ 18-21 in (46-53 cm)
27-42 lb (12-19 kg)

★ *These dogs must have enough exercise—boredom leads to bad habits*

★ *Prone to joint problems*

TEMPERAMENT

Highly intelligent and eager to please, Border Collies are easily obedience trained, but harsh training can make them submissive. They are wonderful pets, especially in homes with energetic children, but can be scrappy and jealous with other dogs.

GROOMING

Regular combing and brushing keeps the coat gleaming, with extra care needed when the soft, dense undercoat is shedding. Bathe or dry shampoo only when necessary. Check the ears and coat for ticks. They can be difficult to locate in the thick undercoat.

AUSTRALIAN SHEPHERD

Highly regarded by farmers as an outstanding working dog long before its recognition as a breed, the Australian Shepherd is not yet widely appreciated beyond this sphere.

 Keen, obedient, loyal

 Minimal

 Regular, vigorous

 Adapts to urban living, but needs plenty of space and exercise

 Good watchdog

 19-23 in (48-58 cm)
40-70 lb (18-32 kg)

 18-22 in (46-56 cm)
35-65 lb (16-29 kg)

★ They are sensitive to some heartworm preventatives

★ Need plenty of exercise, or some real work, to stay in shape

TEMPERAMENT

Extremely intelligent, easily trained, obedient and very responsive these dogs were originally developed in the United States on ranches to work as herding dogs. They seem to know exactly what is required of them.

GROOMING

The Australian Shepherd's coat is easy to groom and needs little attention. Brush occasionally with a bristle brush and bathe only when necessary.

A medium-sized dog, the Aussie, as it is known, has a lean, muscular body and medium-to-long coat, feathered on the ears, chest and underbody and the tops of the legs with a thick ruff on the chest and neck. The tail is short or missing.

Well-proportioned and compact, the Bearded Collie looks like a small Old English Sheepdog. The harsh, long double coat comes in gray, slate, black, red, brown and fawn, sometimes with white. It has a silky beard and feathering.

BEARDED COLLIE

The friendly, even-tempered Bearded Collie is an attractive pet, but is a big commitment for owners as it needs plenty of exercise and grooming and is fairly long-lived.

 Energetic, alert, playful

 Daily brushing

 Regular, vigorous

 Adapts to urban living, but needs plenty of exercise

 Good watchdog

 21-22 in (53-56 cm)
45-55 lb (20-25 kg)

 20-21 in (51-53 cm)
40-50 lb (18-23 kg)

★ If not discouraged early on, Bearded Collies tend to bark a lot

★ May react badly to certain heartworm preventatives

TEMPERAMENT

Intelligent, responsive and fearless, Bearded Collies are willing workers with stamina and endurance. They love children, but due to their size and herding instinct they may frighten a small child.

GROOMING

Daily brushing of the long, shaggy coat is important. Mist the coat lightly with water before you begin then tease out mats. Give more attention when shedding. Use the comb sparingly. The coat can be professionally machine clipped every two months or so. Bathe or dry shampoo when necessary. It is hard to locate ticks in the thick undercoat, so check often.

119

COLLIE

Instantly recognizable to generations of children who were brought up watching the television series "Lassie," the Collie is now one of the most popular dogs in the world.

 Independent, good natured, energetic

 Regular brushing

 Regular, moderate

 Adapts to urban living, but needs plenty of exercise

 Good watchdog

 24-26 in (61-66 cm)
60-75 lb (27-34 kg)

 22-24 in (56-61 cm)
50-65 lb (23-29 kg)

★ *May be sensitive to some heartworm preventatives. Check with your veterinarian*

★ *Subject to some eye problems*

TEMPERAMENT

Sociable and dependent on human company, Collies can be aloof with strangers. They are family oriented and good with children. Intelligent and easy to train, they make good watchdogs but can be terrible barkers.

GROOMING

The spectacular stiff coat sheds dirt readily. A weekly brushing will maintain good condition. Take extra care when the undercoat is being shed. Clip out mats and bathe or dry shampoo as necessary.

A large, strong dog, the Collie often has typical markings of white collar, chest, feet and tail tip. The main colors of the long, thick double coat are sable, tricolor, white and blue merle. The Collie's head is long and tapered, and its expression is gentle and knowing.

Similar to German Shepherd Dogs, there are four varieties distinguished by their coats. The mostly black Belgian Sheepdog and the black-faced, black-eared Tervuren are longhaired. The Malinois has a black face and ears, but has shorter hair. The Laekenois has similar coloring to the Malinois, but its hair is harsh and wiry.

BELGIAN SHEPHERD DOG

The picture of power and grace, the Belgian Shepherd makes its appearance in several guises, but beneath its skin-deep beauty it is a reliable, hard-working and adaptable animal.

 Obedient, willing, intelligent

 Daily brushing

 Regular, vigorous

 Adapts to urban living, but needs plenty of exercise

 Very good watchdog

 24-26 in (61-66 cm)
65-75 lb (29-34 kg)

 22-24 in (56-61 cm)
60-70 lb (27-32 kg)

★ Thorough training is essential

★ Training should always be firm, patient and consistent, as if it is harsh they will be uncooperative

TEMPERAMENT

Essentially working dogs, Belgian Shepherds are easily trained, reliable and obedient. They make excellent police and guard dogs, as well as alert and loyal pets that thrive on loving companionship.

GROOMING

Brush the shorthaired Malinois and the wiry-coated Laekenois regularly with a firm bristle brush. The longhaired Belgian Sheepdog and Tervuren need daily combing and brushing, with extra care when shedding. Clip out mats, especially in the ruff and on the legs. Clip hair from between toes and the outer ears.

OLD ENGLISH SHEEPDOG

If you have endless patience and lots of time to exercise and groom the Old English Sheepdog, your reward will be a faithful and glamorous companion.

 Intelligent, playful, loyal

 Daily, extensive

 Regular, vigorous

 Adapts to urban living, but needs plenty of space

 Good watchdog

 22-24 in (56-61 cm) From 65 lb (29 kg)

 20-22 in (51 cm) From 60 lb (27 kg)

★ If bored and lonely, these dogs can be mischievous

★ It doesn't take long for the coat to get out of control

TEMPERAMENT

Playful and intelligent, Old English Sheepdogs learn fast. Training must start while they are a manageable size.

GROOMING

The coarse, long-haired coat must be combed and brushed through to the dense, waterproof undercoat at least three times a week or it will become matted and the dog may develop skin and parasite problems. A grooming table will make the job easier. Clip out tangles carefully so as not to nick the skin. Trim around the eyes and rear with blunt-nosed scissors. The coat can be clipped by a professional every two months or so.

A big, hardy, thickset, muscular dog, it has a distinctive low-pitched, loud, ringing bark. The shaggy coat comes in gray, grizzle, blue or blue merle, with or without white markings.

Handsome, well proportioned and strong, German Shepherds must be trained from an early age. The coat most often comes in black with tan, sable or all black, but other colors do occur. The nose is black.

GERMAN SHEPHERD DOG

It seems as if the versatile German Shepherd Dog can be trained to do any job. Admired worldwide for its intelligence and excellence as a guard dog, it seems to thrive on service.

 Fearless, loyal, intelligent

 Daily brushing

 Regular, vigorous

 Adapts to urban living, but needs plenty of space

 Outstanding watchdog

 24-26 in (61-66 cm)
75-95 lb (34-43 kg)

 22-24 in (56-61 cm)
70-90 lb (32-41 kg)

★ These dogs need consistent, firm handling by a strong adult

★ This breed suffers from many genetic diseases

TEMPERAMENT

These dogs seem ever-vigilant. They are both loved and feared, with good reason. They are inclined to be reserved and you must win their friendship, but from then on their loyalty is unquestioned.

GROOMING

Daily combing and brushing of the thick, coarse coat is important, and take extra care when the dog is shedding its dense undercoat. At this time, the dead woolly hair clings to the new hair and must be removed with a slicker brush designed for the task. Bathe or dry shampoo only when necessary.

BRIARD

A gentle giant, the Briard is now becoming better known and appreciated outside its native France, where it is highly regarded as an excellent working dog and devoted pet.

 Gentle, reliable, intelligent

 Regular brushing

 Regular, vigorous

 Adaptable to urban living, but needs plenty of exercise

 Very good watchdog

 23-27 in (58-69 cm)
70-80 lb (32-36 kg)

 21-25 in (53-63 cm)
65-75 lb (29-34 kg)

★ The herding instinct is strong

★ Generally healthy, although hip dysplasia and cataracts do sometimes occur

TEMPERAMENT

A long history of working with humans has made Briards sweet natured and gentle. During World War I soldiers were impressed by its abilities as a messenger and by the way it pulled supply wagons. They are intelligent and easy to train, making wonderful family pets and excellent watchdogs.

GROOMING

If the dog is kept outside, the coat seems to largely take care of itself. If the dog spends a lot of time indoors, you may wish to brush the long coat regularly and bathe or dry shampoo as necessary.

A large, muscular animal, the Briard's gait is smooth and looks almost effortless. The long, shaggy coat comes in solid colors, especially black and fawns, the darker the better. The hind legs have double dewclaws.

Primarily a working dog, the Bouvier is powerful and short in the body. The rough, long, shaggy double coat comes in black, gray, brindle, salt and pepper, and fawn, sometimes with a white mark on the chest. A thick beard and mustache adorn the face. The tail is usually docked.

BOUVIER DES FLANDRES

Everything about the Bouvier des Flandres says dependability—from its workmanlike body to its steady manner. Today, it is a police dog and guide for the blind.

 Stable, loyal, obedient

 Regular brushing

 Regular, moderate

 Adapts to urban living, but needs plenty of exercise

 Excellent watchdog

 23-28 in (58-71 cm)
75-90 lb (34-41 kg)

 22-27 in (56-69 cm)
60-80 lb (27-36 kg)

★ These dogs can be suspicious of strangers

★ Rarely ill but may suffer from hip dysplasia or cataracts

TEMPERAMENT

Adaptable and even tempered, the Bouvier goes about its business quietly and calmly. It is easy to train and is an excellent watchdog.

GROOMING

If the dog is kept outdoors, the harsh, dry coat seems to look after itself, shedding dirt and water easily. If the animal lives in the house, you may wish to brush the long coat regularly and bathe or dry shampoo when necessary. Trim the coat occasionally if necessary.

SPORTING DOGS

SPORTING DOGS, also known as gundogs, were bred to work with hunters in the field. Pointers sniff out game birds, pointing toward them with an upraised leg. Setters also locate game but crouch out of the hunter's line of fire. Spaniels flush out game; retrievers collect killed animals.

Sporting dogs are popular pets. They retain their liveliness, love of exercise and intense loyalty.

COCKER SPANIEL

This attractive dog is smaller than its English cousin but retains the lively, friendly personality for which spaniels are known. The Cocker Spaniel is a most appealing pet.

 Lively, happy, friendly

 Daily brushing

 Regular, moderate

 Adapts to urban living, but needs plenty of space

 Good watchdog

♂ 13-16 in (33-41 cm)
25-35 lb (11-16 kg)

♀ 12-15 in (30-38 cm)
20-30 lb (9-14 kg)

★ *Some dogs may display unprovoked aggression*

★ *Prone to spinal problems and ear infections*

TEMPERAMENT

Intelligent and responsive, the Cocker Spaniel is friendly and good natured. However, some dogs may display unprovoked aggression toward their owners, a condition similar to rage syndrome in English Springer Spaniels.

GROOMING

Some owners prefer the coat long, brushing daily and shampooing often. Others clip the coat to be more functional. Either way, the dog will need regular trimming. When brushing, be careful not to pull out the silky hair.

This strong dog has a compact body. The silky coat is short on the head and long on the body—it may grow to the ground. It comes in black, black and tan, solid colors, particolors, tricolors and roans. The ears are long. The tail is often docked.

This strong dog has a sturdy, compact body covered in silky, medium-length, flat-lying hair. The coat comes in reds, black, golden and liver, as well as particolors and tricolors and occasional roans. The tail is usually docked short.

ENGLISH COCKER SPANIEL

An absolute charmer, the joyous English Cocker Spaniel is one of the most popular house pets in its adoptive country. For good looks and personality, it's the leader of the pack.

 Joyful, affectionate, intelligent

 Regular brushing

 Regular, moderate to vigorous

 Adapts to urban living, but needs plenty of exercise

 Good watchdog

 15-17 in (38-43 cm)
28-34 lb (13-16 kg)

 14-16 in (36–41 cm)
26–32 lb (12–15 kg)

★ Prone to ear infections so check ears regularly

★ Prone to genetic eye diseases

TEMPERAMENT

Energetic, playful and eager to please, the English Cocker Spaniel performs with unbounded enthusiasm, wagging its tail and entire hindquarters furiously. It will certainly alert you to the presence of strangers on your property.

GROOMING

Regular combing and brushing of the coat is vital. Bathe or dry shampoo as necessary. Check the ears for grass seeds and signs of infection. Brush the hair on the feet down over the toes and trim it level with the base of the feet. Trim the hair around the pads, but not that between the toes.

BRITTANY

An agile and vigorous hunter, the French Brittany is admired for its abilities in the field, its grace and charm. Although a companionable pet, it prefers the outdoors.

 Gentle, friendly, energetic

 Regular brushing

 Regular, vigorous

 Adapts to urban living, but needs plenty of exercise

 Good watchdog

 17-21 in (43-53 cm)
35-40 lb (16-18 kg)

 18-20 in (46-51 cm)
30-40 lb (14-18 kg)

★ These dogs love exercise and have great stamina

★ Prone to ear infections and gets cataracts

TEMPERAMENT

Easy to train and handle, the Brittany is a loving and gentle animal, obedient and always eager to please. It is highly active and is an excellent tracker, retriever and natural pointer.

GROOMING

Regular brushing of the medium-length, flat coat is all that is needed to keep it in good condition. Bathe or dry shampoo when necessary. Check the ears carefully, especially when the dog has been out and about in rough or brushy terrain.

The smallest of the French spaniels, the Brittany is well muscled with long legs. The coat is feathered on the ears, chest, underbody and legs. It comes in white with black, orange, brown or liver, tricolors and roans. The tail is short.

A hard worker with stamina and endurance, the Welsh Springer is smaller than its English cousin, with smaller and less feathered ears. The thick, silky coat is straight and always white and rich red. The tail is usually docked.

WELSH SPRINGER SPANIEL

Sociable and intelligent, the Welsh Springer Spaniel adapts to any environment but is in its element with space to run and, if you can manage it, access to somewhere it can swim.

 Sensible, energetic, friendly

 Regular brushing

 Regular, moderate

 Adapts well to urban living, but needs plenty of space

 Good watchdog

 17-19 in (43-48 cm)
40-45 lb (18-20 kg)

 16-18 in (41-46 cm)
35-45 lb (16-20 kg)

★ Without exercise, these dogs can become lazy and fat

★ Prone to ear infections

TEMPERAMENT

Springer Spaniels were used to "spring" forward to flush out game for hunters. Highly energetic, its gentle, patient nature and love of children makes the Welsh Springer an easily trained family pet.

GROOMING

The coat is fairly easy to maintain. It requires only regular brushing with a stiff bristle brush. Extra attention is needed during shedding. Bathe or dry shampoo only when necessary. Check the ears often for grass seeds and signs of infection. Trim the hair between the toes and keep the nails neatly clipped.

ENGLISH SPRINGER SPANIEL

The handsome robust English Springer Spaniel excels in the field at flushing out game, but also makes a delightful pet in the home. It is a spirited and loyal companion.

 Alert, friendly, loyal

 Regular brushing

 Regular, moderate

 Adapts well to urban living, but needs plenty of exercise

 Good watchdog

 19-21 in (48-53 cm)
45-55 lb (20-25 kg)

 18-20 in (46-51 cm)
40-50 lb (18-23 kg)

★ Prone to rage syndrome, an inherited behavioral disorder

★ May develop elbow and hip dysplasia

TEMPERAMENT

A quick learner, the Springer enjoys company, is patient with children and makes a good watchdog. Sadly, it is prone to an inherited behavioral disorder called rage syndrome, which can cause aggression. Before buying a pup, check whether any of its relatives are afflicted.

GROOMING

The coat is fairly easy to maintain. Regular brushing with a stiff bristle brush will keep it looking good. Take extra care when the animal is shedding. Bathe or dry shampoo only when necessary but check the large, heavy ears regularly for signs of infection.

This strong dog has a sturdy, compact body.
The soft, medium-length, flat-lying coat comes
mainly in white with liver or black, with or without
tan markings. The tail is usually docked.

This medium-sized dog is athletic and a strong swimmer. The coat is dense, wavy and totally water resistant; the soft undercoat is oily and the feet are webbed. Water is shed with a shake. The coat varies from dark tan to dark brown.

CHESAPEAKE BAY RETRIEVER

A hardy outdoor type, the Chesapeake Bay Retriever is considered a duck dog without peer, with an extraordinary ability to remember exactly where each bird falls.

 Keen worker, can be aggressive

 Regular brushing

 Regular, vigorous; loves to swim

 Adapts to urban life, needs rural access

 Good watchdog

 23-26 in (58-66 cm)
65-80 lb (29-36 kg)

 21-24 in (53-61 cm)
55-70 lb (25-32 kg)

TEMPERAMENT

These dogs are courageous and intelligent, but can be tricky to train. They have a tendency to be aggressive with other dogs. They need a lot of activity, including swimming, to stay in peak condition.

GROOMING

The dense, harsh shorthaired coat is easy to groom. Brush with a firm bristle brush and bathe only if necessary. Bathing destroys the natural waterproofing of the coat. Water is shed completely with a quick shake, so the dog stays warm and dry.

★ These are strong dogs with a tendency to be territorial, so need firm training and good management

LABRADOR RETRIEVER

Courageous, loyal and hard working, the Labrador Retriever has earned respect for its dedication to duty. However, it is also one of the most popular and loving of family pets.

 Reliable, loving, loyal

 Regular brushing

 Regular, vigorous

 Adapts well to urban life, but needs lots of exercise

 Good watchdog

 22-24 in (56-61 cm)
60-75 lb (27-34 kg)

 21-23 in (53-58 cm)
55-70 lb (25-32 kg)

> ★ If allowed, these dogs can often become obese
>
> ★ Prone to hip dysplasia

TEMPERAMENT

Reliable, obedient and easily trained, Labrador Retrievers are friendly and excellent with children. They crave human attention and need to feel a part of the family. Their nature and intelligence make them suitable for work as police dogs and guide dogs for the blind.

GROOMING

The smooth, shorthaired, double coat is easy to groom. Comb and brush regularly with a firm bristle brush, paying attention to the undercoat. Bathe or dry shampoo only when necessary.

This solid, powerful dog is strong, active and a good swimmer. The tail is thick at the base, round and tapered. The waterproof coat comes in black, yellow, fawn, cream, gold or chocolate, sometimes with white chest markings.

This is a graceful and elegant dog. It has a lustrous coat that comes in any shade of gold or cream with the hair lying flat or gently waved around the neck, shoulders and hips. There is abundant feathering.

GOLDEN RETRIEVER

This dog gets the seal of approval from everyone who has ever owned one. Visualize a happy family around a fire—a Golden Retriever asleep on the hearth completes the picture.

 Calm, affectionate, gentle

 Regular brushing

 Regular, vigorous

 Suits urban living, needs plenty of space

 Good watchdog

 22-24 in (56-61 cm)
60-80 lb (27-36 kg)

 20-22 in (51-56 cm)
55-70 lb (25-32 kg)

★ These dogs shed a fair amount of hair

★ Prone to skin allergies

TEMPERAMENT

These are well-mannered, intelligent and charming dogs. They are easily trained and are always patient with children. They make great family pets or companions. While unlikely to attack, they make good watchdogs, loudly signaling a stranger's approach.

GROOMING

The smooth, medium-haired double coat is easy to groom. Comb and brush with a firm bristle brush, paying attention to the dense undercoat. Dry shampoo regularly, but bathe only when necessary.

IRISH SETTER

This elegant and graceful dog is admired for its lustrous chestnut coat with profuse feathering. Bred for Ireland's marshy terrain, it is lighter and speedier than other setters.

 Lively and affectionate

 Daily combing

 Regular, extensive and vigorous

 Not for apartments, requires space

 Not a good watchdog

 26-28 in (66-71 cm)
65-75 lb (29-34 kg)

 24-26 in (61-66 cm)
55-65 lb (25-29 kg)

★ *Lack of exercise makes this dog restless and hard to train*

★ *Prone to skin problems*

TEMPERAMENT

Like most sporting dogs, Irish Setters are full of energy and high spirits. They are also affectionate, sometimes overwhelmingly. Although they can be difficult to train, being easily distracted, the effort is rewarding for both owner and dog. Training must never be strict.

GROOMING

Daily combing and brushing of the soft, flat, medium-length coat is required to keep it in excellent condition. Keep it free of burrs and tangles. Give extra care when the dog is molting. Bathe or dry shampoo only when necessary.

The Irish Setter's profusely feathered silky coat comes in rich shades of chestnut to mahogany, sometimes with splashes of white on the chest and feet. The ears are long and low-set and the legs are long and muscular.

This elegant dog has a chiselled head. Its flat, medium length, straight coat comes in white, flecked with combinations of black, lemon, liver, and black and tan. There is feathering along the underbody and ears.

ENGLISH SETTER

This reliable hard-working dog has strength, stamina and grace. It seems to have an innate sense of what is expected of a gundog, responding intelligently to each new situation.

 Intelligent, friendly

 Daily combing and brushing

 Regular, vigorous

 Not for apartments, requires space

 Adequate watchdog

 24-26 in (61-66 cm)
60-75 lb (27-34 kg)

 23-25 in (58-63 cm)
55-65 lb (25-29 kg)

TEMPERAMENT

Gentle and high-spirited, these dogs take their duties seriously. When one joins a family, it is quiet and loyal. They are friendly, intelligent and adept at anticipating their owner's wishes. They need plenty of room to run.

GROOMING

Daily combing and brushing of the medium-length, silky coat is vital, with extra care when the dog is shedding. Bathe or dry shampoo only when necessary. Trim the hair on the feet and tail and check the long ears for any signs of infection.

★ *Will become restless if not given sufficient exercise*

★ *Likely to roam if its yard is not securely enclosed*

GORDON SETTER

Larger, heavier and more powerful than its cousins, the Gordon Setter was bred as a pointer and retriever. However, it also makes a delightful pet, though one that loves exercise.

 Intelligent, friendly, loyal

 Regular combing and brushing

 Regular, vigorous

 Not for apartments, requires space

 Adequate watchdog

 24-27 in (61-69 cm)
55-80 lb (25-36 kg)

 23-26 in (58-66 cm)
45-70 lb (20-32 kg)

TEMPERAMENT

Calmer than other setters and more reserved with strangers, the Gordon Setter is an affectionate companion. It is reliable with children and fairly easily trained. Training must never be heavy-handed, as it is important not to break the dog's spirit.

GROOMING

Regular combing and brushing of the soft, flat, medium-length coat is required. Check for burrs and tangles. Give extra care when the dog is shedding. Bathe or dry shampoo only when necessary. Trim the hair on the bottom of the feet and clip the nails.

★ Lack of exercise can make these dogs restless

★ Prone to bloat so feed two or three small meals a day

This breed has great stamina. The silky coat is feathered and is always a gleaming black with tan to reddish mahogany markings. On the face, markings are clearly defined and include a spot over each eye.

These hunting dogs are fast on land and are good swimmers with water-resistant coats. The Shorthaired is black or liver, has white spots or is roan. The Wirehaired's coat is liver, liver and white, or black and white. The tail is docked half way.

GERMAN POINTER

These athletic dogs are all-rounders, able to track wounded game, point and retrieve. The Shorthaired is the older type, but the Wirehaired has a hard-wearing coat. Both make good pets.

 Intelligent, reliable, keen

 Regular brushing

 Regular, vigorous

 Adapts to urban living, but needs plenty of space

 Good watchdog

 22-26 in (56-66 cm)
55-70 lb (25-32 kg)

 21-25 in (53-63 cm)
45-60 lb (20-27 kg)

★ With insufficient work can be bored and hard to manage

★ The Wirehaired has a slightly aggressive trait

TEMPERAMENT

German Pointers are obedient and affectionate, but are better off with an outdoor life and lots of work. The breed has a mind of its own and should not be allowed to get the upper hand. They are good with people, but the Wirehaired can be argumentative with other dogs.

GROOMING

Brush the smooth Shorthaired regularly with a firm bristle brush and rub with a towel for a gleaming coat. Brush the Wirehaired twice a week and thin its coat in spring and fall. Bathe both only when necessary. Check the ears regularly for discharge or foreign bodies. Check the feet also, especially after the dog has been exercising or working.

Wirehaired German Pointer

VIZSLA

Hungary's national dog, the agile Vizsla, was little known elsewhere until after World War II. This excellent gundog is now becoming increasingly popular outside its country of origin.

 Intelligent, affectionate, willing

 Regular brushing

 Regular, vigorous

 Adapts to urban living, but needs plenty of space

 Good watchdog

 22-26 in (56-66 cm)
45-60 lb (20-27 kg)

 20-24 in (51-61 cm)
40-55 lb (18-25 kg)

> ★ Vizslas are jumpers and, if bored, will escape from a yard that does not have a fence that is high enough to contain them

TEMPERAMENT

Although good natured, intelligent and easy to train, the Vizsla is sensitive and needs to be handled gently. It is reliable with children and quickly adapts to family life. It loves to swim and needs a lot of exercise.

GROOMING

The smooth, shorthaired coat is easy to keep in peak condition. Brush with a firm bristle brush, and dry shampoo occasionally. Bathe with mild soap only when necessary. The nails should be kept trimmed.

This handsome, lean, well-muscled dog moves gracefully either at a trotting gait or in a swift, ground-covering gallop. The coat is short and close, rusty gold to sandy yellow in color and greasy to the touch.

This superb hunting dog has a well-proportioned, athletic body. The sleek, close-fitting coat comes in silver-gray to mouse, often lighter on the head and ears. The striking eyes are blue-gray or amber. The tail is usually docked.

WEIMARANER

Given firm handling by a strong adult, the assertive Weimaraner makes a wonderful companion and working dog, but you will need boundless energy to keep up with it.

 Intelligent, obedient, friendly

 Regular brushing

 Regular, vigorous

 Adapts to urban living, but needs plenty of space

 Excellent watchdog

 24-27 in (61-69 cm)
55-70 lb (25-32 kg)

 22-25 in (56-63 cm)
50-65 lb (23-29 kg)

★ This dog requires a lot of exercise to prevent boredom

★ Prone to sunburn on the nose in summertime

TEMPERAMENT

Alert, intelligent and strong-willed, the Weimaraner is a versatile breed that is happiest when occupied with work or engaging tasks. It requires firm and thorough training, makes an excellent watchdog and is good with children.

GROOMING

The smooth, shorthaired coat is easy to keep in peak condition. Brush with a firm bristle brush, and dry shampoo occasionally. Bathe with mild soap only when necessary. A rub over with a chamois will make the coat gleam. Inspect feet and mouth for damage after work or exercise. The nails should be kept trimmed.

NON-SPORTING DOGS

THIS GROUP OF DOGS contains the breeds that do not fit neatly into any other category. Some are placed here because the tasks for which they were developed no longer exist. The Bulldog, for example, was bred for fighting and bull-baiting, pastimes that are now outlawed.

Dogs in this assorted group are some of the most beautiful, intelligent and popular breeds.

BICHON FRISE

It is easy to see why people are enchanted by the fluffy Bichon Frise. It loves to be the center of attention and is always eager to please— altogether a delightful and amusing pet.

 Charming, friendly, alert

 Daily brushing

 Regular, gentle

 Ideal for apartment living

 Good watchdog

 9-12 in (23-30 cm)
7-12 lb (3-5 kg)

 9-11 in (23-28 cm)
7-12 lb (3-5 kg)

> ★ If neglected, the coat quickly becomes a sorry, matted mess
>
> ★ Blocked tear ducts can make the eyes run and stain the coat

TEMPERAMENT

Gregarious, the Bichon Frise is playful, merry and not aggressive to people or other dogs. It is intelligent and easy to train. Play takes care of most exercise needs, though they love a walk and romp in the open.

GROOMING

Daily brushing of the long, soft coat with a stiff bristle brush is essential. The fine, silky hair falls in curls and is usually cut with scissors to follow the contours of the body and brushed out to a soft cloud. Dry shampoo as necessary and bathe once a month. Trim around the eyes and ears with blunt-nosed scissors and clean the eyes meticulously to prevent staining.

This sturdy, confident little dog has a lively, prancing gait and a puffy white coat, sometimes with cream or apricot markings. The eyes are round and dark and the large, round nose is black.

The elegant Dalmatian is of medium size with lean, clean lines. It is well muscled and has a short, hard, dense coat of pure white with well-defined, black or liver-colored spots that are randomly splashed over it.

DALMATIAN

Exuberant and fun-loving, the Dalmatian is an excellent choice for anyone with the time to exercise and train it. Although it turns heads, it is more than a fashion accessory.

 Gentle, sensitive, energetic

 Daily brushing

 Regular, vigorous

 Adapts to urban living, but needs plenty of space

 Good watchdog

 19-23 in (48-58 cm)
50-65 lb (23-29 kg)

 19-23 in (48-58 cm)
45-60 lb (20-27 kg)

★ Prone to bladder stones

★ A puppy's hearing must be checked before purchasing as they are prone to deafness

TEMPERAMENT

Spirited and playful, these dogs adore children and can be trusted with them. They are sensitive, so training takes patience and gentle but firm handling. They like a brisk walk or run and for this reason are not suited to apartment living.

GROOMING

Newborn pups are spotless and markings develop in the first year. The smooth, lustrous, short-haired coat is easy to groom. Comb and brush with a firm bristle brush, and bathe only when necessary.

BOSTON TERRIER

Besides being an excellent watchdog, the Boston Terrier has much to recommend it—easy-care, handy size and a delightful disposition. It is rightly a very popular breed.

 Playful, devoted, fearless

 Daily brushing

 Regular, moderate

 Ideal for apartment living

 Excellent watchdog

♂ 11-15 in (28-38 cm)
15-25 lb (7-11 kg)

♀ 11-15 in (28-38 cm)
15-25 lb (7-11 kg)

★ Bitches often experience difficulties giving birth to their large-headed pups because of their narrow pelvis

TEMPERAMENT

Playful and affectionate, Boston Terriers like to be a part of the family. They are reliable with children, intelligent, easy to train and, despite being relatively small, make excellent household watchdogs.

GROOMING

The smooth, shorthaired, fine, glossy coat is easy to groom. Comb and brush with a firm bristle brush, and bathe only when necessary. Wipe the face with a damp cloth every day and clean the prominent eyes carefully. Check both the ears and eyes for grass seeds. Ticks may also lurk in the ears. The nails should be clipped from time to time.

Boston Terriers are compact and well-muscled dogs. Their faces are unmistakable, with short, wide muzzles, prominent eyes set far apart and short, erect ears. These dogs come in brindle or black with white markings.

The coat comes in red, fawn, brindle or fallow, or white pied with any of these colors. The muzzle is sometimes dark. With a solid, muscular body set on stocky legs, it has a deliberate, waddling gait.

BULLDOG

Bulldogs have come to epitomize determination and the broad-chested stance certainly suggests immovability, if not downright stubbornness—yet they are loving pets.

 Reliable, gentle, kind

 Daily brushing

 Regular, moderate

 Adapts well to urban living

 Very good watchdog

 14-16 in (36-41 cm)
45-55 lb (20-25 kg)

 12-14 in (30-36 cm)
35-45 lb (16-20 kg)

TEMPERAMENT

Absolutely reliable, and although its appearance can be somewhat intimidating, it is among the gentlest of dogs. All the same, it will see off any intruder and few would risk an encounter with a dog brave enough to bait a bull. Exercise these dogs gently because some have small windpipes and can be stressed by exertion.

GROOMING

The smooth, fine, shorthaired coat is easy to groom. Comb and brush with a firm bristle brush, and bathe only when necessary. Wipe the face with a damp cloth every day to clean inside the wrinkles.

★ Bulldogs tend to drool and snore and are prone to chronic respiratory problems

★ Be careful not to overfeed

POODLE

Poodles come in three sizes: Standard, Miniature and Toy. Their woolly hair is not shed. For this reason they are often good pets for people with allergies. Their winning ways are captivating.

 Intelligent, loyal

 Comb and brush daily

 Regular, moderate

 Suit apartments, need exercise

 Good watchdog,

 Miniature
11-15 in (28-38 cm)
15-17 lb (7-8 kg)

 11-15 in (28-38 cm)
15-17 lb (7-8 kg)

 Standard
15-24 in (38-61 cm)
45-70 lb (20-32 kg)

 15-22 in (38-56 cm)
45-60 lb (20-27 kg)

TEMPERAMENT

Considered by many the most intelligent of all breeds, the Poodle is a good watchdog that is seldom aggressive. It loves to play and will feel slighted if left out of family activities but can be jealous of children.

GROOMING

Poodle hair keeps growing and must be washed regularly and clipped every six to eight weeks. Check the ears frequently for mites and pull out hairs if neccesary. The teeth need regular scaling.

★ *When buying a puppy, check for genetic disorders*

★ *Poodles fret if left alone*

Poodles are active and sure-footed with a trotting gait. They come in white, cream, brown, apricot, black, silver and blue. The dense coat is clipped in an all-over natural style or clipped in a number of traditional cuts.

These dogs have a harsh double coat, black, but also gold or other solid colors. The hair is smooth on the foxlike head, elsewhere more erect. The male has a ruff around the neck. Schipperkes are often born without a tail.

SCHIPPERKE

While the agile, hardy and independent little Schipperke is remarkably self-sufficient, it is sociable, adapts well to family life and makes a well-behaved, loyal and loving pet.

 Curious, brave, loyal

 Minimal

 Regular, moderate

 Adapts well to urban life and apartments if given plenty of exercise

 Excellent watchdog

♂ 10-13 in (25-33 cm)
12-16 lb (5-7 kg)

♀ 9-12 in (23-30 cm)
10-14 lb (5-6 kg)

★ *This dog tends to be suspicious of strangers*

★ *Needs daily exercise*

TEMPERAMENT

This plucky little dog backs down for nobody and makes an excellent watchdog. It is alert, curious, and nothing escapes its attention. Undemanding and devoted, it looks on itself as part of the family.

GROOMING

The Schipperke is clean and pretty much takes care of its own grooming, but to keep the medium-length double coat in top condition, comb and brush regularly with a firm bristle brush. Dry shampoo only when necessary.

TIBETAN TERRIER

While it is treasured in its native Tibet as a symbol of good luck, you will cherish your little Tibetan Terrier more for its delightful ways and joyous zest for life.

 Loving, alert, playful

 Regular combing

 Regular, gentle

 Ideal for an apartment, needs exercise

 Good watchdog

 14-16 in (36-41 cm)
18-30 lb (8-14 kg)

 13-15 in (33-38 cm)
16-25 lb (7-11 kg)

★ They are energetic dogs, requiring regular play

★ Can be a finicky eater

TEMPERAMENT

These gentle, engaging animals are easy to train, alert and full of bravado. They will certainly let you know if strangers are around. Nimble and sure-footed, they will jump quite high, so escape-proof your yard.

GROOMING

Comb the long, double coat every second day with a metal comb to keep tangle-free. Take extra care when the dense, fine undercoat is shed twice a year. Bathe or dry shampoo as necessary. Trim around the eyes with blunt-nosed scissors. Check the ears regularly.

This compact little animal comes in white, golden, cream, gray shades, silver, black, particolor and tricolor. The shaggy coat is fine and long, falling over the face. The well-feathered tail is carried proudly curled over the back.

This shaggy little dog has a long topcoat that parts along the spine and falls straight on either side. Gold, cream and honey are the most popular colors, but the Lhasa Apso coat also comes in dark colors and particolors.

LHASA APSO

This bewitching creature seems to be composed entirely of hair, but is neither a toy nor a lapdog. It is a rugged little animal that earns its keep as a companion and watchdog.

 Playful, devoted, alert

 Daily, extensive

 Regular, gentle to moderate

 Ideally suited to apartment living

 Good watchdog

 ♂ 10-11 in (25-28 cm)
14-18 lb (6-8 kg)

 ♀ 9-10 in (23-25 cm)
12-16 lb (5-7 kg)

★ *They need a lot of grooming*
★ *Nervous around strangers*
★ *Do not like to be left alone*

TEMPERAMENT

Adaptable, affectionate and loyal, these hardy dogs thrive on human companionship. They are playful, intelligent and easily trained. Their hearing is acute and they will alert you to any unusual sounds and to the approach of strangers.

GROOMING

The thick undercoat can become matted so daily combing and brushing are vital. Dry shampoo as necessary. A short all-over clip allows for easier care. Check the feet for matting and foreign matter stuck there. Clean the eyes and ears meticulously.

KEESHOND

A natural watchdog, the Keeshond is a great favorite in its native Holland, despite not being considered a purebred. It is a long-lived dog and becomes attached to its owners.

 Gentle, intelligent, devoted

 Daily brushing

 Regular, moderate

 Suits apartment life, needs exercise

 Excellent watchdog

 17-19 in (43-48 cm)
55-65 lb (25-29 kg)

 16-18 in (41-46 cm)
50-60 lb (23-27 kg)

TEMPERAMENT

Reliable, adaptable, easy to care for and loyal to its family, the Keeshond is a natural watchdog and easy to train for other tasks. These dogs need regular activity to stay fit and to avoid putting on weight.

GROOMING

Grooming is not as onerous as you might expect, but daily brushing of the long coat with a stiff bristle brush is vital. Brush with the grain first, then lift the hair with a comb, against the grain, and lay it back in place. Bathe or dry shampoo only when necessary. The dense undercoat is shed twice a year, in spring and fall.

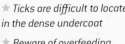

★ Ticks are difficult to locate in the dense undercoat

★ Beware of overfeeding

Keeshonden are compact, muscular dogs with a cream or pale gray undercoat and a luxurious outer coat that comes in shades of gray with black tips and stands away from the body. The markings are definite and there are distinctive pale "spectacles" around the eyes.

The stiff, short, bristly coat feels rough to the touch and comes in black, red, fawn, apricot and cream. The small ears fall forward and the tail is carried in a curl. Like the Chow Chow, these dogs have a blue-black tongue.

CHINESE SHAR PEI

The Chinese Shar pei is thought to be about 2,000 years old. The loose, wrinkled skin gives these dogs an appealingly worried and somewhat forlorn look.

 Amiable, intelligent, independent

 Regular brushing

 Regular, moderate

 Adapts to urban living, but needs plenty of space

 Good watchdog

 18-20 in (46-51 cm)
40-55 lb (18-25 kg)

 18-20 in (46-51 cm)
40-55 lb (18-25 kg)

⭐ *These dogs require a a lot of medical care as many have chronic skin problems and require corrective eye surgery*

TEMPERAMENT

Once used as fighting dogs, the well-mannered Chinese Shar Pei has a surprisingly friendly, easy-going nature and makes a delightful companion, although it may be aggressive toward other dogs and needs to be kept firmly on a leash in public. It needs firm but gentle training and is a good watchdog.

GROOMING

Regular brushing with a bristle brush is enough to keep this dog's unusual coat in good condition. Dry shampoo or bathe when necessary and keep a watchful eye out for mites.

SHIBA INU

Because of its compact size and vivacious, outgoing personality, the Shiba Inu is the most commonly owned pet dog in its native Japan and is gaining in popularity worldwide.

 Energetic, friendly, loyal

 Regular brushing

 Regular, moderate

 Suits urban life or apartment, needs lots of exercise

 Good watchdog

 14-16 in (36-41 cm)
20-30 lb (9-14 kg)

 13-15 in (33-38 cm)
18-28 lb (8-13 kg)

★ Does not like to be left alone

★ Digs and climbs with ease; may wreak havoc as a puppy

TEMPERAMENT

Lively and good natured, Shibas are smart but are independent and choose which commands to obey. They need firm, consistent training. Although extremely sociable, they can be aggressive to unfamiliar dogs.

GROOMING

The coarse, stiff, shorthaired coat is easy to groom. Brush with a firm bristle brush and bathe only when absolutely necessary as this removes the natural waterproofing of the Shiba's coat.

The Shiba is agile and well proportioned
and has a strong body and alert bearing.
The double coat usually comes in red tones,
sable or black and tan, with pale shadings
on the legs, belly, chest, face and tail.

The Chow Chow has almost straight hind legs, which make its walk stiff. Its dense, double coat comes in black, red, fawn, cream, blue or white. It has small, rounded ears, a blue-black tongue and a huge ruff that gives it a lionlike appearance.

CHOW CHOW

An appealing, unusual-looking dog, the Chow Chow is not highly exuberant, but is nevertheless affectionate and loyal. It has a growing band of devotees around the world.

 Reserved, independent

 Regular brushing

 Regular, moderate

 Adapts to urban living, needs space

 Great watchdog

♂ 18-23 in (46-56 cm)
50-65 lb (23-29 kg)

♀ 18-22 in (46-53 cm)
45-60 lb (20-27 kg)

★ Unsuited to hot climates due to its thick coat

★ Be careful around strangers

TEMPERAMENT

The Chow Chow was originally a temple guard and hunting dog. Although strong-willed and something of a challenge to train, it makes an excellent watchdog. It has a reputation for ferocity, probably undeserved, but is a tenacious fighter when it is provoked.

GROOMING

Regular brushing of the long outer coat is important to maintain the lifted, standing-out look. Extra care is needed when the dog is shedding its dense undercoat. Dry shampoo when necessary.

WORKING DOGS

THIS ANCIENT GROUP INCLUDES breeds
that date back to when dogs were used to
guard settlements, carry loads and engage
in battle. Some, such as the Doberman
Pinscher, still make exemplary guard dogs.
Others, such as the Saint Bernard, are
used in rescue work.

*Working dogs are usually large,
strong and obedient. They are loyal
and intelligent family pets.*

AKITA

In Japan, many champions of this breed are considered national treasures. The handsome and much-loved Akita is renowned for its strength, courage and loyalty.

 Brave, affectionate, loyal

 Regular brushing

 Regular, moderate

 Adapts to urban life; needs space and plenty of exercise

 Excellent watchdog

 26-28 in (66-71 cm)
75-120 lb (34-54 kg)

 24-26 in (61-66 cm)
75-110 lb (34-50 kg)

★ *Once a fighting dog, it may be aggressive with other dogs*

TEMPERAMENT

Despite the ferocity of many of its past activities, with diligent training the Akita can make an excellent pet. Care should always be taken around other dogs. The Akita likes to dominate and needs a strong, experienced adult to be in charge. It needs plenty of exercise.

GROOMING

The coarse, stiff, shorthaired coat requires significant grooming and sheds twice a year. Brush with a firm bristle brush. Bathe only when absolutely necessary as bathing removes the natural waterproofing of the coat.

The well-proportioned, muscular Akita has a waterproof double coat that comes in all colors with clear, dark markings. The thick tail is carried in a curl or double curl over the back. Akitas have webbed feet and are strong swimmers.

These are powerful, compact working dogs. The underbody and face marking is always white, while the remaining coat may be light gray to black, gold to red and liver. The plumed tail is carried over the back.

ALASKAN MALAMUTE

This handsome and friendly breed makes a loyal, affectionate family pet. With its strong, powerful body and enormous stamina, it is ideal for work in the Arctic.

 Gentle, friendly, good-natured

 Regular brushing

 Regular, vigorous

 Adapts well to urban living, needs space

 Not a good watchdog

 24-26 in (61-66 cm)
80-95 lb (36–43 kg)

 22-24 in (56-61 cm)
70-85 lb (32-38 kg)

★ May be aggressive with other dogs

★ Unsuited to hot climates

TEMPERAMENT

Malamutes are active and exceptionally friendly to people but not to other dogs. They look intimidating, but are not good watchdogs. They jump and dig, so build a good fence.

GROOMING

Brush the dense, coarse coat twice a week, with extra care during shedding—the undercoat comes out in clumps twice a year. Bathing is mostly unnecessary, as the coat sheds dirt readily. Dry shampoo occasionally.

SAMOYED

The Samoyed is almost always good-humored and ready for a challenge. With its pale, luxurious coat and thick, perky tail curled over the back to one side, it is a spectacular pet.

 Gentle, friendly, good-natured

 Brush regularly

 Regular, moderate

 Adapts to urban living, but needs plenty of space

 Not a good watchdog

 21-24 in (53-61 cm)
45-60 lb (20-27 kg)

 19-21 in (48-53 cm)
45-60 lb (20-27 kg)

TEMPERAMENT

The Samoyed is too friendly to be a watchdog, although its bark will alert you to the presence of strangers. It willingly adapts to family life and gets on well with children. Start training at an early age.

GROOMING

Brushing two or three times a week is usually all that is needed, but extra care is necessary when the dog is shedding. The woolly undercoat comes out in clumps twice a year. Bathing is difficult and mostly unnecessary, as the coat sheds dirt readily. Dry shampoo from time to time by brushing unscented talcum powder 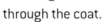 through the coat.

> ★ It is hard to find ticks in the dense, woolly undercoat
>
> ★ Digs holes in order to cool off

The compact muscular body of this hard-working breed shows its strength. The thick, silver-tipped coat comes in white, biscuit and cream.

These are strong and compact working dogs. The mask and underbody are usually white, and the remaining coat any color. Mismatched eyes are common. The big "snow-shoe" feet have hair between the toes for grip on ice.

SIBERIAN HUSKY

A member of the Spitz family, the Siberian Husky is able to haul heavy loads over vast distances in impossible terrain. Noted for its speed and stamina, it is often chosen for polar expeditions.

 Playful, friendly, good-natured

 Brush regularly

 Regular, vigorous

 Adapts to urban living, needs space

 Not a good watchdog

 ♂ 21-23 in (53-58 cm) 45-60 lb (20-27 kg)

 ♀ 20-22 in (51-56 cm) 35-50 lb (16-23 kg)

★ *Lack of exercise makes these dogs restless; if not securely enclosed, they will go off hunting by themselves*

TEMPERAMENT

Because they are friendly and bark little, these huskies are ineffective watchdogs, but their wolflike appearance may deter intruders. Docile and affectionate, they enjoy family life and are dependable around children.

GROOMING

Brush the coarse, medium-length coat twice a week. The woolly undercoat comes out in clumps twice a year and requires extra care. Bathing is difficult and is usually unnecessary, as the coat sheds dirt. An occasional dry shampoo should be enough to keep the coat clean. Clip the nails regularly.

SAINT BERNARD

Admired for feats of rescue in the Swiss Alps, the huge Saint Bernard is strong, sure-footed and seems to have a sixth sense about impending danger from storms and avalanches.

 Placid, affectionate, loyal

 Daily brushing

 Regular, moderate

 Suited to urban living if exercised

 Good watchdog

 27 in (69 cm) or more
110-180 lb (50-81 kg)

 25 in (63 cm) or more
110-180 lb (50-81 kg)

TEMPERAMENT

Dignified and reliable, the Saint Bernard is good with children, in spite of its size. It makes a good watchdog, its size alone being an effective deterrent. It is intelligent and easy to train; however training should begin early, while the dog is still a manageable size, as an unruly dog of this size is a problem for even a strong adult.

GROOMING

Comb and brush with a firm bristle brush, and bathe only when necessary with mild soap—shampoo may strip the coat of its water-resistant oils. During spring and fall, there is considerable shedding. The eyes may water and need special attention to keep them clean and free of irritants.

★ These dogs drool a lot

★ May have eyelids that don't meet properly

These large, strong dogs have rough or smooth dense coats that come in white with markings in tan, mahogany, red, brindle and black in various combinations. They have a highly developed sense of smell.

This is a huge dog with a solid, muscular body. The long, coarse outer coat is straight or slightly wavy; the fine undercoat is soft and thick. The waterproof coat is solid white or has patches of tan, gray or pale yellow.

GREAT PYRENEES

The Great Pyrenees is a truly majestic dog that always impresses, but is a big commitment. You must have the space, patience and, most important, time to meet all its needs.

 Gentle, obedient, loyal

 Regular brushing

 Regular, extensive

 Adapts well to urban life, needs lots of space and exersice

 Very good watchdog

 27-32 in (69-81 cm)
From 100 lb (45 kg)

 25-29 in (63-74 cm)
From 85 lb (38 kg)

★ These dogs don't reach maturity until two years old
★ Prone to deafness

TEMPERAMENT

Although it is gentle and has a natural instinct for guarding, the Great Pyrenees must be well trained while young and small. It needs regular and vigorous exercise to stay fit and healthy.

GROOMING

Regular brushing of the long double coat will keep it in good condition, but extra care is needed when the dog is shedding its dense undercoat. The outer coat does not mat, so care is relatively easy. Bathe or dry shampoo only when necessary.

NEWFOUNDLAND

A naturally powerful swimmer, the Newfoundland has an outstanding record of sea rescues. It was prized by fishermen in its region of origin, along the east coast of Canada.

 Intelligent, gentle, loyal

 Daily brushing

 Regular, moderate

 Adapts well to urban living, but needs plenty of space

 Good watchdog

 27-29 in (69-74 cm)
130-150 lb
(59-68 kg)

 25-27 in (63-69 cm)
100-120 lb
(45-54 kg)

★ Unsuited to hot climates because of its thick coat

★ Some genetic heart conditions

TEMPERAMENT

Famous as the "Nana" dog in *Peter Pan*, these dogs are renowned for being gentle with children. They are adaptable, loyal and courageous, with great strength and endurance. Train when small and easy to manage.

GROOMING

Daily brushing of the thick, coarse, double coat with a hard brush is vital. The undercoat is shed once or twice a year, when extra care is required. Avoid bathing unless absolutely necessary, as this strips away the coat's natural oils. Instead, dry shampoo from time to time.

This massive dog comes in black, browns, or black with white markings—this variant is known as the Landseer after its depiction in a painting by Sir Edwin Landseer. Like some other water-loving breeds, it has webbing between the toes.

A large, powerful dog, the handsome Bernese is vigorous and agile. It has a gleaming, soft, wavy black coat with white and chestnut markings.

BERNESE MOUNTAIN DOG

Once used as a working dog in its native Switzerland, the Bernese Mountain Dog adapts easily to domestic life if it is given plenty of loving attention from the whole family.

 Placid, cheerful, loving

 Daily brushing

 Regular, moderate

 Adapts well to urban life, needs exercise

 Excellent watchdog

 24-28 in (61-71 cm)
85-110 lb (38-50 kg)

 23-27 in (58-69 cm)
80-105 lb
(36-48 kg)

TEMPERAMENT

These gentle, cheerful dogs love children. They are intelligent, easy to train and are natural watchdogs. They are loyal and may have trouble adjusting to a new owner after they are 18 months old.

GROOMING

Daily brushing of the long, thick, silky coat is important, with extra care needed when the dog is shedding. Bathe or dry shampoo as necessary.

★ Prone to hip and elbow dysplasia

★ Inherits eye diseases

BULLMASTIFF

Despite its size and aggressive looks, the Bullmastiff is a devoted family pet and a watchdog par excellence. It rarely barks, never loses its temper and is easy to train and control.

 Placid, gentle, loyal

 Daily brushing

 Regular, moderate

 Adapts well to urban living, but needs plenty of space

 Excellent watchdog

 25-27 in (63-69 cm)
110-133 lb
(50-60 kg)

 24-26 in (61-66 cm)
100-120 lb
(45-54 kg)

★ In public, these dogs should be kept on a leash held by a strong adult

★ They crave human attention

TEMPERAMENT

Although the Bullmastiff is unlikely to attack, it will catch an intruder, knock him down and hold him. At the same time, it is tolerant of children, intelligent, even-tempered, calm, loyal and craves attention.

GROOMING

Comb and brush the shorthaired, slightly rough coat with a firm bristle brush and shampoo only when necessary. There is little shedding with this breed. Check the feet regularly because they carry a lot of weight, and trim the nails.

Smaller and more compact than the Mastiff, the Bullmastiff has a dense, coarse water-resistant coat. It comes in dark brindle, fawn and red, sometimes with white chest markings. The face and neck are darker and deeply folded.

This large, powerful dog has a shorthaired coat that is dense, coarse and lies flat. It comes in shades of apricot, silver, fawn or darker fawn brindle. The muzzle, ears and nose are black and the eyes set wide.

MASTIFF

Few intruders would venture onto a property guarded by a Mastiff, but this imposing dog also has a gentle side and, if properly handled, is utterly devoted to its own people.

 Reliable, brave, can be aggressive

 Regular brushing

 Regular, moderate

 Adapts to urban living, needs space

 Outstanding watchdog

 ♂ From 30 in (76 cm) From about 160 lb (72 kg)

♀ From 27 in (69 cm) From about 150 lb (68 kg)

★ Firm but gentle training is needed to keep this large dog under control

TEMPERAMENT

An exceptional guard dog, the Mastiff must be handled firmly and trained with kindness if it is to be kept under control. Properly handled, it is docile, good natured and loyal, but it can become a big problem if it gets the upper hand.

GROOMING

The smooth, shorthaired coat is easy to groom. Brush with a firm bristle brush and wipe over with a piece of toweling or chamois for a gleaming finish. Dry shampoo or bathe when necessary.

ROTTWEILER

Strong and substantial, the Rottweiler is not for the average home nor for inexperienced owners. It makes an imposing guard dog, but needs firm handling and proper training.

 Courageous, intelligent, reliable

 Brush occasionally

 Regular, vigorous

 Adapts well to urban living, but needs plenty of exercise

 Great watchdog

 24-27 in (61-69 cm)
95-130 lb (43-59 kg)

 22-25 in (56-63 cm)
85-115 lb (38-52 kg)

★ *These formidable animals need kind and consistent training from a strong adult to be kept under control*

TEMPERAMENT

Rottweilers are prized for their aggression and guarding abilities, yet can, with firm handling, also be loyal, loving and rewarding companions. They are highly intelligent and have proved their worth beyond question in police, military and customs work over many centuries. Training must begin young, while the dog is still small, and great care should be taken to ensure that the dog is not made vicious.

GROOMING

The smooth, glossy coat is easy to groom. Brush with a firm bristle brush, and bathe only when necessary.

Compact, muscular dogs, Rottweilers have surprising speed and agility. The thick, medium-length coat conceals a fine undercoat and is black with rich tan to mahogany markings. The tail is usually docked at the first joint.

Great Danes are large, tall, muscular dogs. Their size alone is impressive. They come in fawn, striped brindle, black, blue and harlequin.

GREAT DANE

Ancestors of this aristocratic breed have been known in Germany, where they probably originated, for more than 2,000 years. They are surprisingly gentle for their size.

 Gentle, loyal, affectionate

 Daily brushing

 Regular, moderate

 Adapts well to urban living, but needs plenty of space

 Very good watchdog

 30-34 in (76-86 cm)
120-160 lb
(54-72 kg)

 28-32 in (71-81 cm)
100-130 lb
(45-59 kg)

★ Prone to bloat, so avoid exercise after meals

TEMPERAMENT

Gentle, loyal, affectionate, playful and patient with children, the Great Dane is well behaved and makes a good watchdog—its size alone is daunting. Start training before it gets too large.

GROOMING

The smooth, shorthaired coat is easy to groom. Comb and brush with a firm bristle brush, and dry shampoo when necessary. Bathing this giant is a major chore, so it pays to avoid the need by daily grooming. The nails must be kept trimmed.

BOXER

If your best friend is a Boxer, you can rely on it to absolutely take care of your property and to be waiting with the most enthusiastic welcome whenever you return home.

 Lively, loving, loyal

 Brush occasionally

 Regular, vigorous

 Adapts well to urban living, but needs plenty of space

 Excellent watchdog

 22-24 in (56-61 cm)
60-70 lb (27-32 kg)

 21-23 in (53-58 cm)
55-65 lb (25-29 kg)

★ These dogs need a strong, energetic owner to play with

★ May be aggressive with other dogs

TEMPERAMENT

Intelligent and easily trained, Boxers have been widely used in military and police work. Training should start young and be firm and consistent—these exuberant animals need to be handled by a strong adult. They are reliable and protective with children and intensely loyal to their family. Excellent watchdogs, they will restrain an intruder in the same way a Bulldog does.

GROOMING

The Boxer's smooth, shorthaired coat is easy to groom. Brush with a firm bristle brush and bathe only when necessary.

The body is compact and powerful and the shiny, close-fitting coat comes in fawn, brindle and various shades of red, with white markings. The tail, and occasionally the ears, are docked.

This dog is elegant, muscular and powerful. It has a well-proportioned chest, a short back and a lean, muscular neck. Its close-fitting coat comes in black, black and tan, and more rarely blue-gray, red and fawn.

DOBERMAN PINSCHER

Originally developed to deter thieves, the Doberman Pinscher is prized as an obedient and powerful watchdog. With proper training from puppyhood, it can be a devoted pet.

 Intelligent, loyal, fearless

 Brush occasionally

 Regular, vigorous

 Adapts to urban life if given enough exercise

 Superb watchdog

 26-28 in (66-71 cm)
66-88 lb (30-40 kg)

 24-26 in (61-66 cm)
66-88 lb (30-40 kg)

★ Can become aggressive if not trained from an early age

★ Prone to heart problems

TEMPERAMENT

This breed's reputation for aggression is generally undeserved, but firm and determined training from puppyhood is essential. Fortunately, they are easy to school and make loyal and obedient watchdogs. As well as being fearless, they are alert, agile and energetic. They are powerful animals that should always be watched around young children.

GROOMING

The smooth, shorthaired coat is easy to groom. Comb and brush with a firm bristle brush, and shampoo only when necessary.

SCHNAUZER

Known outside its native Germany for less than a century, the square-looking Schnauzer now has admirers worldwide, who are attracted to its high spirits, stamina and loyalty.

 Spirited, lively, affectionate

 Daily brushing

 Regular, moderate

 Adapts to urban life, needs exercise

 Excellent watchdog

 Standard
18-20 in (46-51 cm)
30-45 lb (14-20 kg)

 17-19 in (43-48 cm)
30-40 lb (14-18 kg)

 Giant
26-28 in (66-71 cm)
60-80 lb (27-36 kg)

 23-26 in (58-66 cm)
55-75 lb (25-34 kg)

TEMPERAMENT

These dogs are reliable, affectionate and are excellent watchdogs. Intelligent and independent, they need firm, consistent training as they can be headstrong. They can be aggressive with strangers.

GROOMING

The coat needs daily grooming to stop matting. Clip out knots then use a short wire brush to brush first with the grain then against. In spring and fall, have the dog professionally clipped all over to an even length. Trim around the eyes and ears with blunt-nosed scissors. Clean the whiskers after meals.

★ *The ears are often cropped in the US; this is illegal in Britain*

The Schnauzer's wiry double coat comes in black or salt and pepper, sometimes with a white chest. The eyebrows and mustache are often trimmed to accentuate the dog's square-cut shape. The tail is often docked. The feet are round and compact.

TOY DOGS

MINIATURE DOGS WERE developed by ancient Chinese emperors as palace companions and lap dogs. They have remained favorites with royalty through the ages. Today they are popular as pets around the world, especially in cities where living space is at a premium.

Toy dogs are often suited to apartment living due to their size and gentle temperament.

CHIHUAHUA

Adored by its owners, the intriguing Chihuahua is prized for its tiny size. Not the best dog for young children, this dainty, bright-eyed creature is perfect for apartment dwellers.

 Affectionate, alert, playful

 Regular brushing

 Regular, gentle

 Ideal for apartment living

 Poor watchdog

 6-9 in (15-23 cm)
2-6 lb (1-3 kg)

 6-8 in (15-20 cm)
2-6 lb (1-3 kg)

TEMPERAMENT

The Chihuahua is intensely loyal and becomes very attached to its owner to the point of jealousy. When strangers are present, it follows its owner's every move, keeping as close as possible. It learns quickly and responds well to training.

GROOMING

The shorthaired coat should be gently brushed occasionally or wiped over with a damp cloth. The long coat should be brushed daily with a soft bristle brush. Bathe about once a month, taking care not to get water in the ears. Check the ears regularly. Keep the nails trimmed.

> ★ These dogs tend to snap out of fear, so be especially careful when handling

*This is the smallest breed of dog in the world.
The two coat types, smooth and short, or long,
can occur in the same litter, although in Britain,
the two are never interbred. Every coat color and
color combination occurs.*

Lithe and streamlined, these dogs are capable of short bursts of speed. The satiny coat comes in various shades of fawn, cream, white, red, blue, black and fawn, and white splashed with any of these colors.

ITALIAN GREYHOUND

A graceful and delicate-looking dog, the Italian Greyhound is a miniature of its larger forebear. A clean, odorless dog, it will adapt happily to any reasonably quiet, loving home.

 Obedient, loving, sensitive

 Minimal

 Regular, moderate

 Adapts to urban living if kept in a quiet household

 Not a good watchdog

 12-15 in (30-38 cm)
6-10 lb (3-5 kg)

 12-15 in (30-38 cm)
6-10 lb (3-5 kg)

★ Prone to broken legs and slipped kneecaps

★ Prone to seizures and inherited eye problems

TEMPERAMENT

As it tends to be timid and must be handled gently, this is a pet for a quiet household where there are no lively children. In stressful situations it needs constant reassurance by stroking.

GROOMING

This dog is one of the easiest to groom. All that is needed to keep the fine, silky coat gleaming is a rubdown with a piece of rough toweling or chamois. If absolutely necessary, the animal can be bathed, but make sure it is thoroughly dry and warm afterward.

CHINESE CRESTED

If you are looking for a novelty pet, the Chinese Crested may be for you, but only if you are ready to return the affection this dainty dog is so eager to give.

 Lively, gentle, devoted

 Frequent grooming

 Regular, gentle

 Ideal for apartment living

 Not a good watchdog

 9-13 in (23-33 cm) Up to 12 lb (5 kg)

 9-13 in (23-33 cm) Up to 12 lb (5 kg)

★ The Hairless is allergic to wool and is easily sunburned

★ Don't feed bones as they have an incomplete set of teeth

TEMPERAMENT

Chinese Cresteds tend to become very attached to their owners and have difficulty adjusting to new ones. They crave constant companionship. Do not overfeed these dogs as they easily become obese.

GROOMING

Daily combing and brushing of the long, fine, double coat of the Powderpuff is important, with extra care required when the dog is shedding. The woolly undercoat becomes matted if neglected. Bathe the Hairless frequently and massage a little oil or cream into the skin to keep it supple.

The two varieties of this dog can be born in one litter. The Hairless, shown below, has hair only on its head, feet and tail. The Powderpuff, at left, has a long, soft coat. Both types come in many colors and can be solid, mixed or all-over spotted.

The Cavalier is slightly larger than the King Charles, with a longer muzzle. The long, silky coat is sometimes wavy and comes in solid reds, chestnut and white, black and tan, and black, tan and white. The long ears are feathered.

CAVALIER KING CHARLES SPANIEL

A fearless, lively little dog with a cheerful nature, the Cavalier King Charles Spaniel is friendly and sociable with both people and other dogs, and is hardier than most toy breeds.

 Lively, friendly, playful

 Regular brushing

 Regular, gentle

Ideal for apartment living

Adequate watchdog

 12-13 in (30-33 cm)
10-18 lb (5-8 kg)

 12-13 in (30-33 cm)
10-18 lb (5-8 kg)

TEMPERAMENT

The Cavalier is easily trained, clean and sensible, and makes a delightful and diverting companion. A romp in the park is enough to provide good exercise.

GROOMING

The smooth, longhaired coat is easy to groom. Comb or brush with a firm bristle brush. Bathe or dry shampoo as necessary. Always make sure the dog is thoroughly dry and warm after a bath. Check the eyes and ears carefully and regularly for any signs of infection.

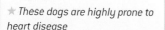 These dogs are highly prone to heart disease

 Prone to ear infections

JAPANESE CHIN

The lovely little Japanese Chin is a dog to dote on and will gladly return the love that is unfailingly lavished upon it. It is a superlative lapdog with few, if any, flaws or vices.

 Intelligent, lively, gentle

 Daily brushing

 Regular, gentle

 Ideal for apartment living

 Poor watchdog

♂ 7-11 in (18–28 cm) Up to 9 lb (4 kg)

♀ 7-11 in (18-28 cm) Up to 9 lb (4 kg)

★ Matted hair must be clipped off the feet
★ Prone to eye problems

TEMPERAMENT

The engaging little Chin is a lively, happy, sweet-tempered dog, the perfect size for small living spaces. With its gentle ways and charming manners, it is perhaps best suited to homes in which there are no small children.

GROOMING

Although the coat looks difficult, a few minutes each day will keep it beautiful. Comb out tangles and brush lightly, lifting the hair to leave it standing out a little. Dry shampoo occasionally and bathe only when necessary. Clean the eyes daily and check the ears regularly for signs of infection.

The Japanese Chin looks like a toy. The profuse, straight, long coat comes in white with markings either of black or shades of red. The Chin's gait is graceful with the feet lifted high off the ground.

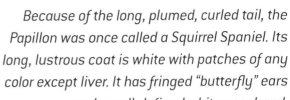

Because of the long, plumed, curled tail, the Papillon was once called a Squirrel Spaniel. Its long, lustrous coat is white with patches of any color except liver. It has fringed "butterfly" ears and a well-defined white noseband.

PAPILLON

The dainty elegance and amusing antics of the Papillon steal hearts. It loves to be the center of attention and enjoys being fussed over. It makes a lovely companion or family pet.

 Animated, friendly, alert

 Daily brushing

 Regular, gentle

 Ideal for apartment living

 Not a good watchdog

 8-11 in (20-28 cm)
8-10 lb (4-5 kg)

 8-11 in (20-28 cm)
7-9 lb (3-4 kg)

TEMPERAMENT

Intelligent and adaptable, these little dogs have perky, friendly natures, but can become possessive of their owners. As watchdogs, their usefulness is limited by their tiny size, but at least their barking will alert you to unusual noises or the arrival of strangers.

GROOMING

Daily combing and brushing of the long, silky, single coat is straightforward but important. These dogs are usually clean and odorless. Bathe or dry shampoo when necessary. Keep the nails clipped and have the teeth cleaned regularly as they accumulate tartar.

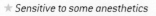

★ Sensitive to some anesthetics

★ Papillons are small enough to wriggle through fences

TOY POODLE

The dainty Toy Poodle loves company. It is the perfect pet for an older or less active person with time to pamper this diminutive natural clown and be amused by its antics.

 Very intelligent, loyal

 Comb and brush daily

 Regular, gentle

 Ideal for apartment living

 Very good watchdog for its size

♂ Up to 11 in (28 cm)
6-9 lb (3-4 kg)

♀ Up to 11 in (28 cm)
6-9 lb (3-4 kg)

★ When buying a puppy, check for genetic disorders

★ This dog prefers indoor life

TEMPERAMENT

Sensitive and remarkably intelligent, the Toy Poodle is highly responsive and easy to train. It makes a wonderful watchdog for its size and is a great companion.

GROOMING

Poodles must be bathed regularly and clipped every six to eight weeks. Clean and check the ears frequently for wax or infection and pull out hairs growing inside the ear canal. Many owners opt for a plain lamb clip, the same length all over, instead of a traditional clip. The teeth need regular scaling.

This active little dog's woolly coat of springy curls keeps growing and is not shed. This means it is often recommended as a suitable pet for people with allergies. The coat comes in red, white, cream, brown, apricot, black, silver and blue.

This compact little dog has a single, silky, dazzlingly white coat that falls long and straight, parting along the spine and eventually reaching the ground and concealing the legs and feet. The tail arches gracefully over the back.

MALTESE

Celebrated since Roman times and perhaps earlier, the main purpose in life of the glamorous little Maltese has always been to lift the spirits of its countless doting owners.

 Even-tempered, affectionate

 Regular, extensive.

 Regular, gentle

 Ideal for apartment living

 Adequate watchdog

 8–10 in (20–25 cm)
4–6 lb (1.5–3 kg)

 8–10 in (20–25 cm)
4–6 lb (1.5–3 kg)

★ The eyes sometimes weep, staining the face

★ Prone to sunburn on the hair parting

TEMPERAMENT

Intelligent and easy to train, the gentle Maltese enjoys being groomed and petted. Lively and alert, it will let you know by barking if strangers are about.

GROOMING

Gentle daily combing and brushing of the long, soft coat is important. Clean the eyes daily and the beard after meals to prevent staining. Bathe or dry shampoo regularly, making sure the dog is dry and warm afterward. Clean the ears and pull out hairs growing in the ear canal. The hair on the top of the head is often tied in a topknot to keep it away from the eyes.

SHIH TZU

Entertaining little dogs that love company, Shih Tzus like nothing better than to sit on a lap and be groomed—which is just as well, because the coat demands extensive care.

 Friendly, playful, independent

 Extensive

 Regular, gentle

 Ideal for apartment living

 Adequate watchdog

♂ Up to 11 in (28 cm)
9-16 lb (4-7 kg)

♀ Up to 11 in (28 cm)
9-16 lb (4-7 kg)

★ Ear infections are common

★ Prone to heatstroke

TEMPERAMENT

With loads of character, the gentle, loyal Shih Tzu makes friends easily and responds well to training.

GROOMING

Daily combing and brushing of the long, soft, double coat with a steel comb and a bristle brush is essential, with extra care needed during shedding. The long hair on the top of the head is usually tied in a topknot to keep it out of the dog's eyes. Dry shampoo as necessary and bathe once a month. Check the ears regularly for infection and remove food scraps from the beard after meals. Clip out any matting on the feet.

This is a proud-looking little dog with a long body and short legs. The long, luxuriant coat can be any color, but a white blaze on the forehead and a white tip on the tail are very desirable.

This little dog looks like a walking powderpuff of black, gray, blue, orange, cream, shaded sable or particolored hair. Its foxlike face peers out from an outsize ruff. The spectacular tail curls over the back.

POMERANIAN

While the Pomeranian adores pampering and petting, it loves to play and be active. In other words, it is an accommodating dog, ready to fit in with the needs of any type of owner.

 Lively, loyal, friendly

 Frequent brushing

 Regular, gentle

 Ideal for apartment living

 Good watchdog despite its size

 7-12 in (18-30 cm)
3-7 lb (1-3 kg)

 7-12 in (18-30 cm)
3-7 lb (1-3 kg)

★ Barking can be a problem if not curbed from an early age

★ Some tooth loss can occur in older dogs

TEMPERAMENT

Easy to train, the happy little Pomeranian makes a good watchdog, despite its tiny size. It will alert you to anything unusual by setting up a commotion. Although excitable, it is obedient and easily calmed.

GROOMING

Frequent brushing of the very long, double coat is needed. Work from the head, parting the coat and brushing it forward; it will fall neatly back in place. The cottony undercoat is shed once or twice a year. Dry shampoo only when necessary. Clean the eyes and ears daily to clear debris. Get regular dental checkups.

PEKINGESE

Venerated since ancient times by the Chinese, the tiny Pekingese is the ultimate lapdog, a devoted companion quite content to loll on a cushion or lap as long as one is available.

 Intelligent, devoted, determined

 Special care is needed

 Regular, gentle

 Ideal for apartments

 Excellent watchdog for its size

 6-9 in (15-23 cm)
10-14 lb (5-6 kg)

 6-9 in (15-23 cm)
10-14 lb (5-6 kg)

TEMPERAMENT

Although small, Pekingese are excellent watchdogs. They are loyal, alert, courageous and good tempered, and fit in well with the family routine.

GROOMING

Daily combing and brushing of the very long, double coat is essential. Take extra care around the hindquarters, which can become soiled and matted. Females shed the undercoat when in season. Dry shampoo regularly. Clean face and eyes daily and check the hairy feet for burrs and objects that stick there.

★ *Eyes are vulnerable to injury and to corneal ulcers*

★ *Breathing problems may require surgery to correct*

These tiny, heavy-boned dogs have a rolling gait. The extravagant, long, flowing coat has profuse feathering and comes in all colors, except albino and liver. The flat face is dark, with a wrinkled muzzle and drooping ears.

The body is small and strong with a silky coat that falls straight on either side of a spinal parting. The coat is long except on the face and ears, and comes in either blue or gray-blue with tan. The tail is often docked.

SILKY TERRIER

Bred purely as a lively companion, the dainty Silky Terrier exhibits the best traits of its several forebears. It is a confident, entertaining little dog with a charm all its own.

 Courageous, alert, affectionate

 Daily, extensive

 Regular, moderate

 Suits apartments, needs exercise

 Excellent watchdog for its size

 9-10 in (23-25 cm)
8-11 lb (4-5 kg)

 9-10 in (23-25 cm)
8-11 lb (4-5 kg)

★ It is an enthusiastic digger

★ Can be jealous and may pick fights with other dogs

TEMPERAMENT

Alert and intelligent, the Silky Terrier is easy to train. It needs plenty of exercise and play to stay fit and healthy.

GROOMING

Grooming this little dog is quite a commitment. Daily combing and brushing and a regular shampoo keep the lustrous hair in top condition. After bathing, make sure the dog is thoroughly dry and warm. The coat must be trimmed occasionally, and the hair on the legs from the knees down is often trimmed short. If the hair that falls over the eyes is tied in a topknot, the dog will find it easier to see.

YORKSHIRE TERRIER

Originally, Yorkshire Terriers were used as ratters, a job they did well. Later, they claimed the spotlight with their unusual appearance and quickly became a favored pet breed.

 Brave, feisty

 Daily, extensive

 Regular, gentle

 Ideal for apartment living

 Good watchdog

 ♂ 7-9 in (18-23 cm)
4-7 lb (2-3 kg)

♀ 7-9 in (18-23 cm)
3-7 lb (1-3 kg)

★ Barking can cause problems with neighbors

★ Scale teeth regularly

TEMPERAMENT

Alert, indomitable and spirited, the Yorkshire Terrier is admired for its loyalty. Despite its tiny size, it makes an excellent watchdog, defending its territory in no uncertain manner. They are not good with children.

GROOMING

For show purposes, there are many tricks to caring for the Yorkshire Terrier's long, single coat and strict guidelines must be adhered to. Many ordinary pet owners opt for a natural shaggy look, but the dog will still need daily combing and brushing and regular shampooing to keep the lustrous hair in top condition. This involves a significant commitment of time and effort.

The ultra-long, fine, silky coat parts along the spine and falls straight down on either side. It is steel-blue on the body and tail, and tan elsewhere. Puppies are mostly black and tan. The tail is usually docked to half its length.

The Pug has a square, thickset, stocky body, a tightly curled tail and a rolling gait. Its sleek coat comes in fawn, apricot, silver and black, all with black muzzle and velvety ears. Moles on the cheeks are considered beauty spots.

PUG

Not at all pugnacious, this lovable softie is even-tempered and good with children. Pugs love company and want to be your best friend, and will sulk if left out of family activities.

 Smart, sociable, mischievous

 Daily brushing

 Regular, moderate

 Suits apartment living if given enough exercise

 Good watchdog

 12-14 in (30-36 cm)
13-20 lb (6-9 kg)

 10-12 in (25-30 cm)
13-18 lb (6-8 kg)

★ A Pug's prominent eyes are prone to injury

★ Prone to sinus and breathing problems

TEMPERAMENT

Intelligent, easily trained, and with a big bark for its size, the Pug makes a good watchdog. It is playful, loyal and affectionate and makes a captivating companion that will shadow your every move or curl up on your lap.

GROOMING

The smooth, shorthaired coat is easy to groom. Brush and comb with a firm bristle brush, and shampoo only when necessary. Clean the creases on the face regularly.

MINIATURE PINSCHER

The Min-Pin, as it is often called, is an active terrier-type of dog. Its courage is undoubted, and it was valued in Germany, where it originated, as a ratting dog of diligence and tenacity.

 Brave, lively, playful

 Daily brushing

 Regular, gentle

 Ideal for apartments, but barking can be a problem

 Excellent watchdog for its size

 10-12 in (25-30 cm)
8-10 lb (4-5 kg)

 10-11 in (25-28 cm)
8-9 lb (about 4 kg)

★ These dogs take off at any opportunity

★ Prone to choke on small objects

TEMPERAMENT

This brave, playful little dog will bark and nip at intruders and, for its size, makes an excellent watchdog. It is not suited to families with small children because, if handled roughly, it is likely to be injured and react aggressively.

GROOMING

The smooth, shorthaired, hard coat is easy to groom. Comb and brush with a firm bristle brush and shampoo only when necessary. Loose hair can be removed by wiping over with a warm, damp washcloth.

This small, neat, lively dog has a characteristic high-stepping gait. The coat comes in black, blue and chocolate, with sharply defined tan markings on the face and chest. Solid reds are also seen. The tail is usually docked short.

TERRIERS

THESE DOGS WERE developed mainly in the British Isles over the past few hundred years, although there are records of small hunting dogs from earlier times. Bred to hunt small game, often digging them out of burrows, they are determined and brave, with short legs and strong jaws.

Much of the aggression has been bred out of terriers. These popular pets often like digging.

CAIRN TERRIER

The vivacious little Cairn Terrier delights with its antics and will steal your heart with its courage and fun-loving ways. It makes an ideal pet and is adaptable, friendly and alert.

 Alert, frisky, friendly

 Regular brushing

 Regular, moderate

 Ideal for apartment living

 Good watchdog

 10-13 in (25-33 cm)
14-18 lb (6-8 kg)

 9-12 in (23-30 cm)
13-17 lb (6-8 kg)

★ Prone to skin allergies

★ Requires considerable attention and maintenance

TEMPERAMENT

Strong, fearless and companionable, the Cairn Terrier is always ready to play or be petted. It will alert you to the presence of strangers by its growling and on-guard stance. This dog is intelligent and easily trained.

GROOMING

The shaggy "natural" look actually takes quite a bit of maintenance. If neglected, its coat soon becomes a sorry, matted mess. Brush several times a week, being gentle with the soft undercoat. Bathe monthly and brush the coat while it dries. Trim around the eyes and ears with blunt-nosed scissors and clip the nails regularly.

This compact little animal has a shaggy, weather-resistant outer coat that comes in cream, wheaten, red, sandy, gray, brindle, black, white or black and tan, with ears and mask often darker. The thick undercoat is soft and furry.

A sturdy, low-set dog, its straight, weather-resistant, double coat comes in blue and rich tan, clear reds or sand shades. The topknot is lighter with a thick ruff. The tail is generally docked.

AUSTRALIAN TERRIER

Although its talents as a rat and snake killer are called on less frequently now, the playful little Australian Terrier retains the best characteristics of a working dog.

 Bold, good-natured, friendly

 Regular brushing

 Regular, gentle

 Ideal for apartments

 Too friendly to strangers to be a good watchdog

 ♂ 9-11 in (23-28 cm) 9-14 lb (4-6 kg)

♀ 9-11 in (23-28 cm) 9-14 lb (4-6 kg)

TEMPERAMENT

Keen and smart, the Australian Terrier responds well to training and makes a delightful pet. It is always eager to please and loves being around children.

GROOMING

The long, stiff, shaggy coat is easy to care for and does not need clipping. Brush several times a week, being gentle with the soft undercoat. Once a month, bathe the dog and brush the coat while it dries. Trim around the eyes and ears, if necessary, with blunt-nosed scissors. Be sure to clip the nails regularly.

★ These dogs are avid hunters

★ Quiet and affectionate, great with children, elderly or the handicapped

NORWICH TERRIER

A feisty, short-legged little dog, the Norwich Terrier has a big heart and is happiest when looking after its human family. It makes a good watchdog and devoted companion.

 Fearless, lively, loyal

 Daily combing and brushing

 Regular, moderate

 Ideal for apartment living, but needs plenty of exercise

 Very good watchdog

 About 10 in (25 cm)
10-13 lb (5-6 kg)

 About 10 in (25 cm)
10-13 lb (5-6 kg)

★ To avoid fights, always keep on the leash when other dogs are around

★ Prone to back problems

TEMPERAMENT

Although good natured and friendly with people, including children, the Norwich Terrier can be scrappy with other dogs and often bears the scars of brief encounters. It is alert, smart and easy to train.

GROOMING

Care of the shaggy, medium-length, waterproof coat is easy, but daily combing and brushing is important. Take extra care when the dog is shedding. Little clipping is required and bathe or dry shampoo only when necessary.

This small working terrier has a sturdy body and short legs. The wiry, straight coat comes in red, tan, grizzle, wheaten, black and tan, sometimes with white marks. The face has whiskers and eyebrows. The tail is usually docked.

This dog has short legs. It is strong, active and agile. The rough-textured, weather-resistant coat comes in black, wheaten or brindle. The undercoat is short, dense and soft. Sharply pricked ears give it a thoughtful look.

SCOTTISH TERRIER

The sturdy, active little Scottish Terrier is so distinctive that it has become an unofficial emblem of its native land. While a little stubborn, it nevertheless makes a wonderful pet.

 Happy, brave, loyal

 Regular brushing

 Regular, moderate

 Ideal for apartment living

 Very good watchdog

 10-11 in (25-28 cm)
19-23 lb (9-10 kg)

 9-10 in (23-25 cm)
18-22 lb (8-10 kg)

TEMPERAMENT

Although somewhat dignified in its behavior, the Scottish Terrier makes a good watchdog. It is inclined to be stubborn, however, and needs firm handling from an early age or it will dominate the household.

GROOMING

Regular brushing of the wiry coat is important and extra care should be taken when the dog is molting. Bathe or dry shampoo as necessary. The dog should be professionally trimmed twice a year. The hair on the body is left long, like a skirt, while the hair on the face is lightly trimmed and brushed forward.

★ Likes to go wandering

★ Prone to skin ailments, including flea allergies

JACK RUSSELL TERRIER

Admired for its courage and tenacity, the Jack Russell Terrier
will take on all challengers. An excellent watchdog, it will also
keep your property free of small interlopers, such as snakes.

 Curious, vigilant,
energetic

 Regular brushing

 Regular, moderate

 Ideal for apartment
living

 Excellent watchdog
for its size

 10-15 in (25-38 cm)
15-18 lb (7-8 kg)

 9-14 in (23-36 cm)
14-17 lb (6-8 kg)

TEMPERAMENT

Jack Russell Terriers are happy, excitable dogs that love to
hunt—they'll chase just about anything that moves. They
make vigilant watchdogs, but are sometimes scrappy with
other dogs. Smart and quick witted, they must be firmly
trained from an early age, but settle well into family life
and make devoted pets.

GROOMING

Both smooth and rough
coats are easy to groom.
Comb and brush regularly
with a firm bristle brush and
bathe only when necessary.

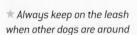
★ Always keep on the leash
when other dogs are around

★ Happiest with space to run

This tough little dog is clean and a good size for a house companion. The coat may be smooth and short, broken (very short wire) or rough and a little longer. It comes in white, or white with black, tan or lemon markings.

This is a sturdy little terrier with a white coat and bright, dark eyes. The ears are small, pointed and erect, giving the animal an alert, ready-for-anything look. The tail is carried jauntily and should not be docked.

WEST HIGHLAND WHITE TERRIER

A perfect mascot or companion, the West Highland White Terrier has charm and vitality, brains and beauty in one neat package. It makes a bright and entertaining pet.

 Adaptive, bright, friendly

 Daily brushing

 Regular, gentle

 Ideal for apartment living, but needs regular exercise

 Good watchdog

 10-12 in (25-30 cm)
15-18 lb (7-8 kg)

 9-11 in (23-28 cm)
13-16 lb (6-7 kg)

TEMPERAMENT

Friendly, playful, alert and self-confident, this dog loves companionship. It is bold, strong and brave, and makes a good watchdog, despite its size.

GROOMING

The harsh, straight, shorthaired double coat sheds very little. Simply brush regularly with a stiff bristle brush to keep the coat clean. Bathe only when necessary. Trim around the eyes and ears with blunt-nosed scissors. The coat needs to be trimmed about every four months and stripped twice a year.

★ Suffer from serious allergic skin problems
★ Keep an eye on these dogs—they are avid hunters

BORDER TERRIER

A plain, no-nonsense little working dog, the Border Terrier is game for anything. It loves being part of a family and is unrestrained in its displays of affection.

 Energetic, affectionate, loyal

 Minimal

 Regular, moderate

 Ideal for urban and apartment living, but needs plenty of exercise

 Good watchdog

 13-16 in (33-41 cm)
13-16 lb (6-7 kg)

 11-14 in (28-36 cm)
11-14 lb (5-6 kg)

★ A bored Border Terrier can become destructive
★ Start gentle training at a very early age

TEMPERAMENT

Reliable and intelligent, Border Terriers are easily trained, obedient, sensible and bright. They are not usually aggressive with other dogs but may hunt your cat and drive it crazy.

GROOMING

The durable, wiry coat needs little grooming. Clip out any knots and brush occasionally with a bristle brush. The object is a completely natural look with no artifice. Bathe only when it is necessary.

The Border Terrier has a wiry double coat. It comes in reds, wheaten, blue and tan, or grizzle and tan. The muzzle and ears are dark. Its loose skin, which feels thick, allows the dog to wriggle into tight burrows. Its head is otter-like.

The Smooth has a flat coat and the Wire's is coarse, dense and broken with a soft undercoat. The dogs are white, with tan or black and tan markings. The V-shaped ears fold and fall forward. The tail is usually docked.

FOX TERRIER

The look and stance of super-alertness and expectation is the hallmark of the Fox Terrier. Wire and Smooth Fox Terriers are remarkably similar in nearly every way, except in their coats.

 Keen, alert, independent

 Regular brushing

 Regular, moderate

 Ideal for urban or apartment living; needs exercise

 Good watchdog

 14-16 in (36-41 cm)
15-20 lb (7-9 kg)

 13-15 in (33-38 cm)
13-18 lb (6-8 kg)

TEMPERAMENT

Keen, boisterous, alert and independent, the Fox Terrier needs to be firmly trained from an early age. It enjoys being part of the family and is reliable with children, although it can be argumentative with other dogs. While Fox Terriers make good watchdogs, the high-pitched barking can be annoying to humans.

GROOMING

Brush the shorthaired coat of the Smooth with a firm bristle brush and bathe or dry shampoo as necessary. Have the Wire professionally groomed if it is a show dog, but keep neat in the same way as the Smooth if the dog is simply a family pet.

★ Fox Terriers are enthusiastic diggers

★ Prone to allergic skin conditions

MINIATURE SCHNAUZER

A dog of clean habits and neat size, the perky Miniature Schnauzer makes a delightful little companion for an apartment dweller or someone with a small house and yard.

 Spirited, lively, affectionate

 Daily brushing

 Regular, moderate

 Ideal for apartment living, but needs plenty of exercise

 Excellent watchdog

 ♂ 12-14 in (30-36 cm)
11-18 lb (5-8 kg)

 ♀ 11-13 in (28-33 cm)
10-15 lb (5-7 kg)

★ The ears are sometimes cropped—this practice is illegal in Britain
★ Prone to cysts

TEMPERAMENT

These dogs are reliable, affectionate and make excellent watchdogs. They are spirited and brave. While not aggressive, they will take on larger dogs.

GROOMING

The wiry coat is reasonably easy to look after. It needs to be combed or brushed daily with a short wire brush to stop matting. Clip out any knots. The animal should be clipped to an even length in spring and fall by a professional. Trim around the eyes and ears with blunt-nosed scissors. Clean the whiskers after meals.

The strong, angular, square-looking Miniature Schnauzer has a wiry double coat in salt and pepper or any solid color, sometimes with white on the chest. The eyebrows and mustache are often trimmed. The tail is usually docked.

The body is flexible and muscular, covered in a thick and slightly curly coat with a woolly undercoat. It comes in blue, liver and sandy beige, or particolored tan with any of these colors. The eyes are dark to light hazel.

BEDLINGTON TERRIER

In full show trim, the Bedlington Terrier looks more like a lamb than a dog, but it has retained its terrier qualities and is a surprisingly fast runner. It makes a devoted companion.

 Alert, intelligent, curious

 Specialized

 Regular, moderate

 Adapts well to urban and apartment life; needs exercise

 Very good watchdog

 ♂ 16-17 in (41-43 cm)
18-23 lb (8-10 kg)

 ♀ 15-16 in (38-41 cm)
18-23 lb (8-10 kg)

★ It is an enthusiastic digger

★ Can be scrappy with other dogs and is a formidable fighter if provoked

TEMPERAMENT

Although they can be stubborn, Bedlington Terriers are affectionate and relatively easy to train. They love to be the center of attention, are devoted companions and make very good watchdogs.

GROOMING

The coat does not shed and requires specialized clipping every six weeks, so it is probably best if you have a professional groomer show you how to do it. The coat is thinned and clipped close to the head and body to accentuate the shape. Shave the ears closely, leaving a tassel on the tips. On the legs, the hair is left slightly longer. Brush the dog regularly and clean and pluck inside the ears to remove debris.

IRISH TERRIER

Known for its fighting spirit, the game little Irish Terrier is not for everyone, but it is adaptable and its courage and loyalty are unquestioned. The breed has a growing band of admirers.

 Intelligent, loyal, brave

 Regular brushing

 Regular, vigorous

 Adapts well to urban living, but needs plenty of exercise

 Excellent watchdog

 16-19 in (41-48 cm)
25–30 lb (11-14 kg)

 15-18 in (38-46 cm)
23-28 lb (10-13 kg)

★ Argumentative with other dogs
★ Keep on a leash when out

TEMPERAMENT

While sociable with people and devoted to its owner, this dog has an often uncontrollable urge to fight with other dogs, and is unsuitable for inexperienced owners.

GROOMING

The hard double coat is easy to groom and rarely sheds. Brush regularly with a stiff bristle brush and remove the dead hair with a fine-toothed comb. Bathe or dry shampoo only when necessary.

The Irish Terrier looks a little like a small version of the Airedale Terrier. Its hard, short and wiry coat comes in solid red, red-wheaten or yellow-red.

This medium-sized dog's stiff, wiry, waterproof coat comes in a dark grizzle or black with red and tan markings. The face has a beard, mustache and eyebrows. The docked tail is carried erect. Small V-shaped ears fold to the sides.

AIREDALE TERRIER

A lively, water-loving medium-sized dog, the Airedale Terrier is highly adaptable and fits in well with family life as long as it has plenty of exercise and is not allowed to rule the roost.

 Reliable, loyal, lively

 Regular brushing

 Regular, moderate

 Adapts well to urban living, but needs plenty of exercise

 Good watchdog

 23-24 in (58-61 cm)
40-50 lb (18-23 kg)

 22-23 in (56-58 cm)
40-45 lb (18-20 kg)

★ These dogs are incorrigible diggers and are easily bored, so keep them occupied

★ Prone to skin infections

TEMPERAMENT

Airedales are intelligent, reliable and loyal dogs. They are not difficult to train, but they do not respond well to harsh or overbearing methods. They are naturally lively and love playing with children.

GROOMING

The Airedale's hard, shorthaired, double coat is easy to groom and sheds very little. Brush regularly with a stiff bristle brush to remove the dead hair and bathe only when necessary.

BULL TERRIER

Although surprisingly gentle, the Bull Terrier is a powerful and determined animal. It needs firm handling. Even the Miniature is not a dog for timid or inexperienced owners.

 Determined, fearless, playful

 Regular brushing

 Regular, moderate

 Adapts well to urban life; needs space and exercise

 Excellent watchdog

 Standard
21-22 in (53-56 cm)
52-56 lb (23-25 kg)

21-22 in (53-56 cm)
45-60 lb (20-27 kg)

 Miniature
Up to 14 in (36 cm)
Up to 20 lb (9 kg)

 Up to 14 in (36 cm)
Up to 20 lb (9 kg)

TEMPERAMENT

A tenacious fighter, the Bull Terrier is more of a danger to other dogs than to people. When properly trained it is usually sweet natured, gentle and playful. Some dogs, however, suffer from obsessive compulsive behaviors, such as tail chasing.

GROOMING

Brush with a firm bristle brush, and bathe or dry shampoo as necessary. The coat will benefit from a rub down with a piece of toweling or chamois.

★ May be aggressive with other dogs
★ Some pups are born deaf

A thick-set, muscular dog, the Bull Terrier has a short, dense coat that comes in pure white, black, brindle, red, fawn and tricolor. Its distinctive head is almost flat at the top, sloping evenly down to the nose. The small eyes are closely set.

Substantial, well-proportioned and muscular, the Staffordshire has a short, dense coat that comes in white or solid reds, fawn, brindle, black or blue, or any of these colors with white.

STAFFORDSHIRE BULL TERRIER

A trustworthy all-purpose dog, the Staffordshire Bull Terrier is intelligent and affectionate, good with children and an excellent watchdog that will intimidate any intruder.

 Tough, brave, reliable

 Daily brushing

 Regular, moderate

 Adapts to urban living, but needs plenty of exercise

 Excellent watchdog

 14-16 in (36-41 cm)
25-38 lb (11-17 kg)

 13-15 in (33-38 cm)
23-35 lb (10-16 kg)

TEMPERAMENT

Usually adored and adoring within its own family circle, the Staffordshire needs firm and consistent training to curb its instinct to fight with other dogs. As pups, they tend to chew a great deal so make sure you provide them with plenty of chew toys. They love exercise.

GROOMING

The smooth, shorthaired coat is easy to groom. Brush every day with a firm bristle brush, and bathe or dry shampoo as necessary. The coat will gleam if rubbed with a piece of toweling or chamois.

★ To avoid fights, must be leashed in public

★ Can overheat in hot weather

AMERICAN STAFFORDSHIRE TERRIER

Stoic and reliable, the American Staffordshire Terrier is a dog few strangers would mess with, yet in its own family, this powerful animal is devoted, gentle and loving.

 Tough, reliable, courageous

 Daily brushing

 Regular, moderate

 Adapts well to urban living, but needs plenty of exercise

 Excellent watchdog

 17-19 in (43-48 cm)
40-50 lb (18-23 kg)

 16-18 in (41-46 cm)
35-45 lb (16-20 kg)

TEMPERAMENT

The American Staffordshire should never be confused with the notorious Pit Bull Terrier. Although it is a courageous and tenacious fighter if provoked, and needs firm, kind training to control this instinct, its basic temperament toward people is gentle and loving.

GROOMING

Brush the smooth shorthaired coat daily with a firm bristle brush. Bathe or dry shampoo as necessary. Rub with a towel or chamois to make the coat gleam.

★ *To avoid dog fights, keep leashed in public*

★ *May develop cataracts*

The American Staffordshire looks much like the British, although it is larger overall. It probably bears an even closer resemblance to Bulldogs of a century ago, from which it is descended. The coat comes in all colors.

This strong, medium-sized dog has great stamina. The soft single coat is long and wavy and does not shed. It comes in wheaten shades. The face has a beard and mustache, with hair falling over the eyes. The tail is usually docked.

SOFT-COATED WHEATEN TERRIER

A jolly creature, the Soft-coated Wheaten Terrier seems to retain its carefree puppy ways into adulthood. Its enthusiasm and zest for life make it a delightful companion and pet.

 Exuberant, friendly, fearless

 Daily grooming

 Regular, moderate

 Adapts well to urban living

 Excellent watchdog

 18-20 in (46-51 cm)
35-45 lb (16-20 kg)

 17-19 in (43-48 cm)
30-40 lb (14-18 kg)

TEMPERAMENT

Friendly and appealing, the Wheaten is intelligent and easy to train. It makes an excellent watchdog.

GROOMING

Daily combing of the long, profuse coat with a medium-toothed comb is recommended to keep it free of tangles, beginning when the dog is a puppy. The object is to achieve a natural look and brushing can make the soft coat fuzzy. Clean the eyes and check the ears carefully. Bathe or dry shampoo when necessary.

★ These dogs need regular exercise and play to stop them from getting bored

★ Prone to skin infections

HOUNDS

DOGS FROM THIS GROUP are among the most ancient. First developed to chase down and kill large prey, many are capable of great speed and stamina. They are divided roughly into sighthounds and scent hounds, depending on how they locate their prey.

Used as police dogs or for racing, hounds make good pets but need plenty of exercise.

BASSET HOUND

The mournful face of this gentle, lovable hound belies its lively nature. When hunting, it is single-minded, but it makes a delightful pet in homes where there are young children.

 Gentle and loyal

 Weekly brushing, paying attention to ears and feet

 Regular, moderate

 Suited to urban living

 Not a good watchdog

 12-15 in (30-38 cm)
50-65 lb (23-29 kg)

 11-14 in (28-36 cm)
45-60 lb (20-27 kg)

TEMPERAMENT

Good-natured, sociable and gentle with children, Basset Hounds fit into family life well. With proper training, they are obedient, but when they pick up an interesting smell, it is sometimes hard to get their attention—a reflection of their hunting heritage.

GROOMING

The smooth, shorthaired coat sheds moderately. Comb and brush with a firm bristle brush and shampoo only when necessary. Wipe under the ears every week and trim toenails regularly.

★ These dogs may smell due to skin and ear infections

★ Prone to overeating and becoming fat

*This sturdy, long, barrel-shaped dog has short,
stocky legs on which the skin is loose and folded.
The shorthaired coat comes in combinations of
white with tan, black and, occasionally, lemon.
The ears are long and velvety.*

This squat, muscular dog is the smallest of the pack hounds. Its dense waterproof coat comes in combinations of white, black, tan, red, lemon and blue mottle.

BEAGLE

It's not only its manageable size that makes the Beagle so popular. It is endearing and engaging, eager to romp and demanding little of its owner's time for grooming or exercise.

 Alert, joyful, even-tempered

 Regular brushing

 Regular, moderate

 Adapts well to urban living

 Not a good watchdog

 14-16 in (36-41 cm)
22-25 lb (10-11 kg)

 13-15 in (33-38 cm)
20-23 lb (9-10 kg)

TEMPERAMENT

Beagles need firm handling as they are strong willed and not always easy to train. When they pick up an interesting smell, it is sometimes hard to get their attention. Alert, good tempered and craving companionship, they are rarely aggressive and love children.

GROOMING

The Beagle's smooth, shorthaired coat is easy to look after. Brush with a firm bristle brush. Bathe with mild soap only when necessary. Check the ears carefully for signs of infection and keep the nails trimmed.

★ Beagles bay when they bark, which can be irritating

★ They are prone to wander

DACHSHUND

These extraordinary "sausage" dogs come in a range of colors, sizes and coat types—it seems there's a sturdy little Dachshund for every taste, but most owners have preferences.

 Brave, curious, lively

 Regular brushing

 Regular, moderate

 Ideal for apartment living

 Good watchdog

 Standard
About 8 in (20 cm)
16-32 lb (7-15 kg)

 About 8 in (20 cm)
16-32 lb (7-15 kg)

 Miniature
About 6 in (15 cm)
Up to 11 lb (5 kg)

 About 6 in (15 cm)
Up to 11 lb (5 kg)

TEMPERAMENT

Alert, lively and affectionate, Dachshunds are good company and reasonably obedient when carefully trained. They can be slightly aggressive to strangers and have a loud bark for their size. Miniatures are less suited to households with young children, as they are vulnerable to injury from rough handling.

GROOMING

Regular brushing with a bristle brush is appropriate for all coat types. Dry shampoo or bathe when necessary. Always make sure the dog is dry and warm after a bath. Rub the smooth variety with a towel or a chamois. Check the ears regularly.

> ★ Prevent these dogs from becoming obese as they are prone to spinal damage
> ★ Enthusiastic diggers

Both Miniature and Standard Dachshunds have
a low-slung, muscular, long body with short legs
and strong forequarters. The skin is loose and
the coat can be smooth, longhaired or wirehaired.
They come in a range of colors and patterns.

The Whippet's lean, delicate appearance belies its strength and speed—it can accelerate rapidly to about 35 mph (55 km/h). The fine, dense coat comes in many colors and mixes. The muzzle is long and slender.

WHIPPET

Gentle, affectionate and adaptable, the Whippet is a delightful companion and jogging partner. Clean and well behaved in the house, it settles happily into family routine.

 Sensitive, gentle, high strung

 Brush occasionally

 Regular, moderate

 Adapts to urban living, but needs plenty of space

 Not a good watchdog

 19-22 in (48-56 cm)
20-22 lb (9-10 kg)

 18-21 in (46-53 cm)
19-21 lb (9-10 kg)

★ These dogs can be nervous and must be handled gently

★ The bones are easily broken

TEMPERAMENT

Gentle and sensitive, the Whippet makes a surprisingly docile and obedient pet, although it is inclined to be nervous when lively children are around. While it is easily trained, owners must take great care not to break its spirit by being harsh or overbearing during training.

GROOMING

The smooth, fine, shorthaired coat is easy to groom. Brush with a firm bristle brush. Bathe only when necessary. A rub all over with a damp chamois makes the coat gleam. Keep the nails clipped.

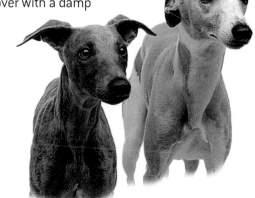

GREYHOUND

Agile and fleet, this breed is one of the oldest known breeds, long valued for its hunting prowess. The Greyhound's lean, elegant lines are often found on coats of arms of royalty.

 Docile, loving and sensitive

 Groom occasionally

 Regular, moderate

 Adapts well to urban life if exercised

 Good watchdog

 28-30 in (71-76 cm)
65-70 lb (29-32 kg)

27-28 in (68-71 cm)
60-65 lb (27-29 kg)

★ Should be leashed in public

★ May be sensitive to some common anesthetics and flea-killing products

TEMPERAMENT

Gentle and sensitive, the Greyhound makes a docile and obedient pet. However, it retains a highly developed chase instinct and should always be kept on a leash in public. Greyhounds are good with children and settle happily into family routine. While these dogs are easily trained, owners must be careful not to break their spirit by being harsh or overbearing during training.

GROOMING

The smooth, shorthaired coat is easy to groom. Brush with a firm bristle brush. Shampoo only when necessary. A rub with a chamois will ensure that the coat gleams.

Lean and powerful, these dogs are built for speed. Their long legs can propel them at up to 45 mph (70 km/h). The short, fine coat comes in black, gray, white, red, blue, fawn, fallow, brindle or any of these with white.

The Basenji is a compact, muscular, medium-sized dog with a trotting gait. The loose, silky, shorthaired coat comes in combinations of white, tan, chestnut, brindle and black. When alert, it wrinkles its brow. The tail is curled over the back.

BASENJI

A handsome, muscular dog, the Basenji is a fastidious groomer, even washing itself with its paws. Although the breed is known for being barkless, it "yodels" when it is happy.

 Intelligent, playful, independent

 Weekly brushing

 Regular, vigorous

 Well suited to urban living

 Poor watchdog

 16-17 in (41-43 cm)
22-26 lb (10-12 kg)

 15-16 in (38-41 cm)
20-25 lb (9-11 kg)

TEMPERAMENT

Alert, affectionate, energetic and curious, the Basenji loves to play and makes a good pet, as long as it is handled regularly from an early age. It is very intelligent and responds well to firm but consistent training.

GROOMING

The smooth, shorthaired, silky coat is easy to groom. Comb and brush with a firm bristle brush. Bathe or shampoo only when necessary.

★ Provide them with plenty of chew toys

★ They like to climb fences

AFGHAN HOUND

While undeniably elegant and beautiful in peak condition, the Afghan Hound is not an easy-care pet. Choose one only if you are prepared to make a big commitment in time.

 Independent, lively, loving

 Extensive

 Regular, vigorous

 Adapts to urban living, but needs plenty of space

 Not a watchdog

 ♂ 26-29 in (66-74 cm)
55-65 lb (25-29 kg)

 ♀ 24-26 in (61-66 cm)
45-55 lb (20-25 kg)

★ *These dogs require a great deal of grooming and exercise*

TEMPERAMENT

Although they are intelligent, Afghan Hounds are not easy to train and, being large, they are not easy to handle either. They are definitely not a fashion accessory and owners need to establish a genuine relationship with them. Too many of these dogs have been abandoned due to unrealistic expectations of owners who have underestimated the time needed to care for them.

GROOMING

The long, thick coat demands a great deal of attention and must be thoroughly brushed every day. Dry shampoo when necessary and bathe once a month.

The coat is very long, straight and silky, except on the face and along the spine. Thick falls of hair on the legs keep it warm. It comes in all colors and some combinations. The end of the tail should curl in a complete ring. The gait is free and springy.

A tall, elegant dog, the Borzoi has a lean, muscular body designed for speed. The long, wavy, silky coat is profusely feathered, and is usually white with colored markings. The small ears are pointed and well feathered.

BORZOI

The well-mannered Borzoi is a dog of grace and is dignified and gentle. If you want a constant companion and can give it the exercise and love it craves, this may be the dog for you.

 Gentle, reserved, sensitive

 Regular brushing

 Regular, moderate

 Adapts well to urban life; needs exercise

 Not a good watchdog

 At least 28 in (71 cm)
75-105 lb (34-48 kg)

 At least 26 in (66 cm)
60-90 lb (27-41 kg)

★ Borzois need a well-padded bed to prevent calluses and irritation to elbows

TEMPERAMENT

Gentle, reserved and sometimes nervy around children, Borzois are affectionate with their owners and tolerant of other dogs, but they need plenty of attention.

GROOMING

The long, silky coat is easy to groom. Brush regularly with a firm bristle brush, and dry shampoo when necessary. Bathing presents problems with such a tall dog but shouldn't be required very often. Clip the hair between the toes to keep the feet comfortable and to stop them from spreading.

SALUKI

This ancient breed was used in Arabia for hunting gazelle and other game. Slim, fine-boned and athletic, they are capable of bursts of speed up to 40 mph (65 km/h) and great endurance.

 Gentle, loyal and sensitive

 Brush twice weekly

 Regular, moderate

 Adapts well to urban living if exercised

 Not a good watchdog

 23-28 in (58-71 cm)
50-60 lb (23-27 kg)

 20-27 in (51-69 cm)
35-55 lb (16-25 kg)

TEMPERAMENT

Gentle, affectionate and intensely loyal, Salukis quickly become part of the family, although they may be aloof with strangers. They are not aggressive but can be rather sensitive and, while easy to train, they become nervous and timid if the trainer's manner is overbearing or harsh.

GROOMING

The soft, smooth, silky coat is easy to groom and there is little shedding. Comb and brush with a firm bristle brush, and shampoo only when necessary. Be careful not to overbrush as this may break the coat. Trim the hair between the toes or it will matt and make the feet sore and uncomfortable.

★ These dogs are able to jump very high fences

★ Cancer is a growing problem for this breed

There are two types of coat, smoothhaired and feathered, both with feathering on the ears and tail. The soft, smooth, silky coat comes in black and tan, white, cream, fawn, gold and red, as well as various combinations of these.

Large and powerful, the Bloodhound looks tougher than it is. The skin is loose and the coat is short and dense and comes in tan with black or liver, tawny, or solid red. There is sometimes a little white on the chest, feet and the tip of the tail.

BLOODHOUND

Brought to England by William the Conqueror, the solemn-looking Bloodhound has entered literature and legend as the archetypal sleuth dog, but it never kills its prey.

 Gentle, sensitive affectionate, shy

 Minimal

 Regular, vigorous

 Adapts to urban living; needs space and exercise

 Not a good watchdog

 25-27 in (63-69 cm)
90-110 lb (41-50 kg)

23-25 in (58-63 cm)
80-100 lb
(36-45 kg)

★ A bored Bloodhound's mournful howl may not be enjoyed by neighbors

★ Prone to ear infections

TEMPERAMENT

Sensitive, gentle and shy, a Bloodhound becomes devoted to its master and gets along well with people and other dogs; despite its reputation, it is rarely vicious.

GROOMING

The smooth, shorthaired coat is easy to groom. Brush with a firm bristle brush, and bathe only when necessary. A rub with a rough towel or chamois will leave the coat gleaming. Clean the long, floppy ears regularly.

RHODESIAN RIDGEBACK

An all-weather, low-maintenance, dedicated watchdog, the Rhodesian Ridgeback bonds closely with its adoptive family in the early years of its life and makes a devoted, fun-loving pet.

 Brave, gentle, loyal

 Daily brushing

 Regular, moderate

 Adapts well to urban living, but needs plenty of space

 Outstanding watchdog

 25-27 in (63-69 cm)
80-90 lb (36-41 kg)

24-26 in (61-66 cm)
65-75 lb (29-34 kg)

★ Training should be gentle and start while the dog is small enough to manage

★ Beware of overfeeding

TEMPERAMENT

Like many powerful dogs, the Rhodesian Ridgeback is a gentle, friendly animal, although it can be a tenacious fighter when aroused. It makes an outstanding watchdog and a devoted family pet. Intelligent and good natured, it is easy to train, but should be treated gently so as not to break its spirit or make it aggressive.

GROOMING

The smooth, shorthaired coat is easy to groom. Brush with a firm bristle brush and shampoo only when necessary.

This is a strong, active dog with a dense, glossy coat that comes in solid shades of red to light wheaten with a dark muzzle and sometimes a little white on the chest. When alert, the brow is somewhat wrinkled.

A massive, muscular dog, the Irish Wolfhound is the tallest breed in the world. Its rough, wiry coat comes in gray, brindle, red, black, fawn and white. The paws are large and round, with markedly arched toes and strong, curved nails.

IRISH WOLFHOUND

A true gentle giant, the Irish Wolfhound is affectionate and wonderful around children. It was once used to hunt wolves—so successfully that wolves disappeared from the British Isles.

 Calm and gentle

 Daily combing

 Regular, moderate

 Needs plenty of space; unsuited to apartments

 Adequate watchdog

 32-38 in (81-95 cm)
115-125 lb
(52-57 kg)

28-32 in (71-81 cm)
100-110 lb
(45-50 kg)

★ To avoid joint damage, do not take young dogs for long walks

★ Can be rather difficult and expensive to look after

TEMPERAMENT

In spite of being a killer of wolves, this dog is gentle, loyal and very affectionate. It is trustworthy around children, although it might knock them over with its large tail. While disinclined to bark, its size alone should be daunting to intruders.

GROOMING

Unless the hard, wiry coat is combed often, it will become matted. Clip out any knots. Trim around the eyes and ears with blunt-nosed scissors.

NORWEGIAN ELKHOUND

Surprisingly, the handsome Norwegian Elkhound can adapt to warmer climates than its homeland as the thick coat insulates it from both heat and cold. It makes a fine pet.

 Fearless, intelligent, good-tempered

 Regular brushing

 Regular, vigorous

 Adapts to urban living, but needs plenty of exercise

 Good watchdog

 19-21 in (48-53 cm)
50-60 lb (23-27 kg)

 18-20 in (46-51 cm)
40-55 lb (18-25 kg)

TEMPERAMENT

While gentle and devoted to its owner, the Elkhound needs consistent training that is firm but never harsh. Although adaptable, it likes a set routine.

GROOMING

Regular brushing of the hard, coarse, weatherproof coat is important, with extra care when the dog is shedding its dense undercoat. At this time, the dead hair clings to the new hair and must be removed with a rubber brush designed for the task. Bathing is largely unnecessary.

★ *Their thick coats require a lot of grooming*

★ *Needs lots of exercise*

Silent while tracking, this dog makes a range of vocal sounds. It has a thickset body with a tightly curled tail. The coat comes in grays with black tips and lighter hair on the chest underbody, legs and underside of the tail. There is a neck ruff.

INDEX

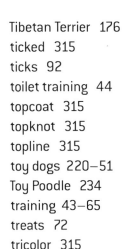

ACKNOWLEDGMENTS

All maps and illustrations © Weldon Owen Pty Ltd. All photographs © Weldon Owen Pty Ltd except 8-35, 42-43, 46-70, 72-76tr, 77-87, 92tr, 94-99, 102-103, 104br, 107br, 108br, 111br, 102br, 106br, 110br, 124br, 127br, 128br, 131br, 132-34br, 137br, 138br, 141br, 142br, 143, 145br, 146br, 150br, 153br, 154br, 158br, 162-164, 167br, 168br, 172br, 176br, 179br, 184br, 188-90br, 193br, 197br, 201br, 202br, 205br, 206br, 209br, 213br, 214br, 217br, 218br, 220-222br, 229br, 230br, 234br, 237br, 238br, 242br, 245br, 246br, 249br, 250br, 252-53, 254br, 262br, 265br, 266br, 270br, 274br, 277br, 281br, 282br, 285br, 286-288br, 291br, 296br, 299br, 300br, 303br, 307br, 311br istockphoto.com; 92bl, 93, 255, 259, 264 Getty Images; 257br Wikipedia